𝓑OB SCHULTZ

BOYHOOD
ᴬ𝒩ᴰ BEYOND

Practical Wisdom for Becoming a Man

Scripture quotations are taken from the King James Version of the Bible.

Boyhood and Beyond: Practical Wisdom for Becoming a Man
Copyright © 2004 Bob Schultz

Text Illustrations by Emily Schultz
Cover Design by Alpha Advertising
Interior Design by Pine Hill Graphics

Library of Congress Cataloging-in-Publication Data
(Provided by Cassidy Cataloguing Services, Inc.)

   Schultz, Bob.

      p. ; cm.

   1. Boys--Spiritual life. 2. Young men--Spiritual life. 3. Spiritual life.
4. Christian education of boys. 5. Christian education of young people.
I. Title.

Printed in the United States of America.

To Janet

Introduction

When the publishers asked me to write a book for boys and young men, I laughed. So did my wife and daughters. I've never had sons.

The publishers encouraged me to use my own life experience and my understanding of God's Word, and this book is what came out of that effort. It's simply a review of lessons God has used as He leads me in manhood.

I hope these chapters encourage you to become the man God wants you to be and help you to see God in the people and world around you. And though you may never put your experiences down on paper, He is writing a book upon your heart. It is the story of God wanting to have a relationship with you, His son.

—Bob Schultz

Contents

IF

If you can keep your head when all about you
Are losing theirs and blaming it on you;
If you can trust yourself when all men doubt you,
But make allowance for their doubting too;
If you can wait and not be tired by waiting,
Or, being lied about, don't deal in lies,
Or, being hated, don't give way to hating,
And yet don't look too good nor talk too wise;

If you can dream—and not make dreams your master;
If you can think—and not make thoughts your aim;
If you can meet with triumph and disaster
And treat those two imposters just the same;
If you can bear to hear the truth you've spoken
Twisted by knaves to make a trap for fools,
Or watch the things you gave your life to, broken,
And stoop and build 'em up with worn-out tools;

If you can make one heap of all your winnings
And risk it on one turn of pitch-and-toss,
And lose, and start again at your beginnings
And never breathe a word about your loss;
If you can force your heart and nerve and sinew
To serve your turn long after they are gone,
And so hold on when there is nothing in you
Except the Will which says to them: "Hold on!"

If you can talk with crowds and keep your virtue,
Or walk with kings—nor lose the common touch;
If neither foes nor loving friends can hurt you;
If all men count with you, but none too much;
If you can fill the unforgiving minute
With 60 second's worth of distance run—
Yours is the Earth and everything that's in it,
And—which is more—you'll be a Man, my son!

—Rudyard Kipling

Nature is the chart of God,
marking out all his attributes.

—*The Golden Gems of Life*

A Grand Book

Every day I read from a grand book. It is the oldest book I know. God designed it to be read by every person in the world. It describes what God has done in the past and what He is doing today. The book declares His greatness. Whoever reads it has no excuse for not acknowledging God and His creation and control of the world. The mind of the man who will not believe this book becomes dark. God will turn him over to wickedness.

Do you know the name of this book?

The chapters of this special book can be understood by anyone around the globe. Men read it before they ever learn an alphabet. But no man has ever read it from cover to cover. Of those who have tried, none has successfully read even one quarter of the pages. Some pages are never read.

Now, do you know the title of this book?

Around 1510, a boy named Bernard Palissy was born in France. His life offers an outstanding example of industry and diligence. Bernard purposed to discover the secrets of covering pottery with porcelain. With no one to instruct him, he guessed and tried. When he failed, which he did over and over, he tried again. After sixteen weary years, he fulfilled his dream and became a famous potter, respected by kings. At age seventy-eight, Bernard Palissy died in a Paris prison, refusing to deny his Lord Jesus.

When Palissy began his education, his family did not own a single book. "I had no other books," he said afterward, "than heaven and earth which were open to all."

This grand book that I have been asking you about is called heaven and earth. No one can afford to own the volume, yet it is open for even the poorest to read and receive instruction.

Why did God make boys so that they like to climb, dig, camp, hike, and explore? He wanted boys to discover Himself in the middle of His grand book. Instead of sitting at a desk reading about the world, He gave them the energy and will to swim in it, crawl under it, and jump around on it. He gave boys the desire to turn over rocks, pick up bugs, and catch fish. Boys like to build forts, net butterflies, and wade through creeks. Only a creative teacher can hold a young boy's attention when there is life to explore outdoors.

What can the grand book of heaven and earth teach a boy? First, it can teach him to work. "Go to the ant, thou sluggard," says the old proverb, "consider her ways, and be wise: which having no guide, overseer, or ruler, provideth her meat in the summer, and gathereth her food in the harvest." A careful study of insects reveals a world of hard workers. The honey bees have much to teach about the sweet rewards of diligent work. You will not be wasting time to spend hours observing these insects. If you remember what you see and apply it to your life, you will grow to be a very wise man.

Second, the heavens and earth teach a boy good manners. One afternoon I sat watching the chickens in their pen. The rooster was an example of a true gentleman. Of course, he wasn't really a gentleman. He was a chicken and a real nuisance at times—that's why we gave him away! However, this particular day he taught me a good lesson. He swaggered around the chicken yard acting like he owned the place. When he found something worth eating, he gave a cluck, which brought the hens running. With his beak, he picked up the morsel, broke it in half, and then threw it back on the ground. The nearest hen gobbled it up. He continued this practice as long as I watched. Sometimes I threw in some corn just to watch his display of self-control and kindness to the hens.

Third, the heavens and earth declare the glory of God. Have you ever gone out on a dark night and gazed at the stars? In these days of electric lights, it is sometimes hard to find a dark clear place to observe the heavens, but with some effort it can be done. In 1605, without the aid of a telescope, Johannes Kepler discovered that the planet Mars had an elliptical orbit around the sun. This discovery came at a time when almost all men were convinced that the earth was the center of the universe. Men also believed that the planets and stars moved in complicated patterns across the sky. Amazingly, after six years of careful observation and mathematical calculations, Kepler proved that the complicated theories of his day were wrong. Mars followed a simple elliptical orbit established by God.

Kepler's discoveries deepened his confidence in God. They gave him strength to stand firm when he was persecuted for his faith. At the close of his book *Harmony of the*

Worlds he wrote, "Great is God our Lord, great is His power and there is no end to His wisdom. Praise Him, you heavens, glorify Him sun and moon and you planets, for out of Him, through Him, and in Him are all things…We know, oh, so little, to Him be the praise, the honor and the glory from eternity to eternity."

Here was a man who read God's wonderful book carefully. He observed the simplicity and orderliness of his God. Kepler's heart knew the security of living in a world created and governed by an orderly and loving God. Any book which can do that for you is worth careful study!

If you want to understand God's ways, go out and observe His handiwork. Look at the birds. Why is the male bird usually clothed with brilliant colors and the female bird usually the color of a nearby shrub? What does that show of God's protection? Watch the seasons. Why did God create them? Why does a grain of wheat die before it bears fruit? How and why does God use clouds to water the earth? You will grow in your understanding of God and His ways by going outside, observing, asking questions like these, and then carefully searching for the answers. He will fill you with wonder and praise.

The heavens and the earth are not to be worshipped, as some foolish men attempt to do. They are given to lift our hearts out of our selfish perspectives and raise them to heights of praise for what our Creator is.

Don't let this world around you squeeze you into buildings or books. Buildings are good. Books are good. There are times to be in both. But God created the heavens and the earth to be experienced, not just read about or lectured upon.

If you live in the country, make time to observe the life surrounding you. Sit in a barnyard, feel the warmth of the sun, and listen to what the animals can teach. If you live in the city, take advantage of visits or vacations to explore what rural life has to offer.

Even if you live in an apartment, you can still see enough of the heavens and the earth to fill your heart with God's glory. You could set up a bird feeder on your porch or plant a few bean seeds in a large pot on the back deck. Make it a personal goal to harvest some beans before the summer is over. It is not as easy as you may think, and there is much to learn in the process. A microscope could open a chapter of discovery into the protozoan world found in every mud puddle in town. Even the cockroaches

in the pantry declare the glories of God, if we would slow down enough to read their story.

Kepler concluded his book *Cosmic Mystery* with these words, "Thus God himself was too kind to remain idle and began to play the game of signatures, signing his likeness into the world."

You and I have the privilege of playing that game with Him. We can hunt for the signature and likeness of our wonderful God as He writes throughout His creation. Some signatures are easy to spot, like a sunset. Others, like the process of photosynthesis, require intense study to uncover.

God does not give grades for studying the book of the heavens and earth. His reward is to fill His students with wonder and praise. He gives His scholars a sense of security. They understand that He created their world and knows every detail of the universe. Like Kepler, they gain the assurance that God understands them and is attentive to the details and needs of their lives.

His grand book is open in front of you. Go—spend hours and days reading His creation. Let your heart fill to the brim with wonder. Let your mouth praise the glory of our Creator!

> *But ask now the beasts. And they shall teach thee; and the fowls of the air, and they shall tell thee: or speak to the earth, and it shall teach thee: and the fishes of the sea shall declare unto thee* (Job 12:7,8).

Questions

- What was the only book that Palissy had to read when he began his studies?

- Who wrote this book?

- What do you gain if you carefully study the heavens and the earth?

- What chapters of God's creation would you like to discover?

No man is bound to be rich or great—
no, nor to be wise; but every man is bound
to be honest.

—Sir Benjamin Rudyard

Admit It

When I was sixteen, I drove a group of my friends home from an outing. The guys were having a great time throwing things at each other. Something flew by me. Dodging it, I accidentally turned the steering wheel and sideswiped a parked pickup. SLAM! That got everybody's attention.

"Keep going!" someone shouted.

"Don't stop!" yelled another.

"Get out of here!"

"No one will find out," they protested.

I wanted to run. My mind raced through what would happen if I did run. How would I explain the dents on my car? What if I got caught? I stopped to turn around. The clutch was going out and I could hardly get the transmission into reverse. Grinding gears, I headed back. My friends kept shouting, "Don't go back."

Part of me wanted to run, part of me wanted to return. Against the protests, I went to the house where the truck was parked. I rang the bell. When a man came to the door, I said, "I hit your pickup."

"I know you did," he replied.

"I'll do whatever it takes to make it right," I said. Inside I was afraid because I didn't know what it would take to make it right. I knew one thing—I didn't have much money and neither did my parents.

He arranged to take his truck in for an estimate before deciding what to do. When I heard the amount, I confessed that I couldn't pay it all at once. He agreed to accept what I could pay each month. Three months later, I took in the last payment. I remember shaking hands in front of his display counter at the meat market where he worked. What a happy day that was! The agreement was completed. I was free from my wrong, plus I had a new friend.

I learned a lesson that day. The easy way out of trouble is to confess your mistakes.

Twenty-five years later I stood in a huge bathtub gasping for breath. I couldn't believe what I had just done. I was framing on a new house and needed to install some blocking on the wall behind a four-foot-wide fiberglass tub. Stepping into it to reach the blocks, I accidentally dropped the air nailer I carried. It misfired and shot a three-and-a-half-inch nail through the bottom of the tub!

I felt sick. The same wrong thoughts that I faced years before came into my head.

"Don't tell anyone! Hide it. No one will know that you did it." Does it surprise you that an older man would be tempted to hide his mistake? Men, at every age, want to hide their faults, but if we do hide them we are fools.

God's Spirit spoke loudly to my heart, "You can't do that. You must tell the truth the first chance you get. The general contractor comes back in a couple of hours—tell him."

When the contractor did return, I pushed aside my strong desire to hide. Walking quickly to him, I told him my mistake. Now it was his turn to feel sick. He called the plumber, who called the manufacturer. Within minutes, the contractor came to me smiling. He announced, "The tub company has a warranty policy on all of its tubs. Any construction damage they'll fix without charge."

Again, I was free. The easy way out of trouble is to confess your mistakes.

All of your life you will face the temptation to hide your faults and your mistakes. Every man and boy that you know faces that same temptation. You may worry about people getting mad at you. Or you might fear the cost of making it right. Maybe you think about your embarrassment. Don't let any of those thoughts stop you from the freedom that comes with quick confessions. If you do not confess your faults quickly, it will be much worse for you when someone finds out about it later. Then, not only will you be at fault, you will also be labeled as a coward or a cheat.

What do you get if you confess your mistakes quickly? Everyone knows how hard it is to confess faults. Therefore, when you confess yours, others instantly respect you for it. You gain a reputation of being honest. You develop boldness to look fear in the face and say, "Get behind me." When you confess quickly, you cultivate a responsible attitude of paying for your mistakes. You stand tall without any secrets to hide. There's freedom in your heart, mind, and spirit.

Sometimes when you confess your faults, others will still get angry with you. Accept it humbly. Know that you had it coming. Receive the punishment as one who deserved it. Keep your head up. All men make mistakes. Part of manhood is accepting your mistakes and repairing what you can.

Are you willing to try an experiment? The next time you make a mistake, go directly to the one you wronged, admit it, and watch what God will do. Pick up your courage; walk past your fears; speak the truth. It's the man's road to freedom.

> *If we say that we have no sin, we deceive ourselves, and the truth is not in us. If we confess our sins, he is faithful and just to forgive us our sins, and to cleanse us from all unrighteousness* (1 John 1:8,9).

Questions

- Have you ever broken something and feared admitting it?

- Can you remember admitting a fault and finding that you didn't get in as much trouble as you thought you would?

- Does your dad or mom have a story about how they were tempted to hide a fault? What was the result?

- What was the experiment you were encouraged to try?

...Man, proud man,
Dressed in little brief authority,
Plays such fantastic tricks before high heaven
As make the angels weep.

—William Shakespeare

Authority

Her head was gone. The rest of the chicken sat there—but without a head. When a raccoon kills a chicken, he often begins his feast with the head. When he feels full, he leaves the bird as she is, without her head, until the next night. If you find a headless chicken, you can be pretty sure that, one night soon, the raccoon will be back. That's a good time to set a trap if you want to catch him.

Only one chicken with a head remained in my neighbor's chicken house. The raccoon got 'em, one by one. My neighbor Gary took it personally. No raccoon was going to get *all* of his chickens! He began to sleep in a travel trailer parked beside the pen. On the third night he heard it, *Sqwaaaaaaaaaaaak.* That's a dying chicken call. After you hear one, you won't forget it.

Grabbing his .45 caliber pistol, Gary jumped out the door. His appearance startled the raccoon, who let the chicken go. Darkness made it difficult to see clearly, but a shadow sprinted for the spot where the raccoon had entered before. The pistol jerked into action, *Kablooom.* A dead-on shot! Feathers flew everywhere. The raccoon scampered out another hole in the fence and disappeared. Gary stared in disbelief. The raccoon *didn't* get all his chickens. He shot the last one himself.

Gary had authority over his chickens. They were his to do with whatever he wanted. He could feed them, if he wanted. He could cook them, if he wanted. He intended to use his authority and power to protect them. However, Gary's intentions backfired. Instead of protecting his last chicken, he eliminated her. This happens frequently with men. They often use their God-given authority and power to do selfish things. They hurt and kill when they should be helping and saving.

As you grow, you are given authority and you gain power. You receive authority when you are asked to watch your brothers and sisters or when you are given the responsibility of caring for a pet. Your power increases as your muscles develop. With maturing wisdom comes advantage over those with less understanding.

These developing strengths and skills will help you gain a position on a job, or in a church, or in the community. Or perhaps one day you'll marry and have children. These are all areas of authority and power. Will you protect those under your care, or will you hurt them?

God does not give authority so that you can force others to obey your wishes. Authority is the opportunity to use all your skill, all your resources, and all your wisdom to make those under you successful.

Dad and Mom ask Kasey to watch his little brothers and sisters while they go for a walk. Kasey is trusted with authority because he is strong enough to lift the little ones when they need to wash their hands. He is placed in charge because he can use his wisdom to look both ways for cars before crossing the street. His parents count on him because he has the best ability to protect the others and provide what they need for useful and joyful living.

Kasey is mistaken if he thinks his main job is keeping the little ones from doing anything wrong. If he continually says no to this, and no to that, until all they can do is sit on the couch with their hands folded, he is like my neighbor holding a gun on his chicken and shouting, "Don't move!" A skillful babysitter will use his authority to create a pleasant atmosphere while doing things that benefit the whole family.

The best example of good authority versus bad authority is found by comparing Jesus and the Pharisees. Jesus has all authority and power. He always uses that authority for the benefit of people. He is the servant of everyone and uses His resources to meet their needs. Once, even a group of demons asked Jesus for permission to enter a herd of pigs. He granted their request. Jesus does not use His power to push folks around. With His authority He serves.

The Pharisees were the religious leaders in Jesus' day. They are examples of those who use authority selfishly. God gave them authority to teach and lead people to God. The Pharisees lost sight of their purpose. Instead of helping people worship God, they put burdensome laws upon them, drove away all of God's messengers, and even killed Jesus, the One who gave the Pharisees their authority. Almost every time the Pharisees used their power, they were trying to stop someone from doing something. Almost every time Jesus used His power, He was *helping* someone to do something.

The right use of authority says things like this: "Sure, you can do that!" "Here, I have a tool that can help you with your task." "Use this money to buy the material you need." "Go ahead, wade in the river and I will stand downstream in case you fall in." "That's a great idea; I'll help you do it."

27

Some boys have much authority, others very little. Maybe you have only one thing to be in charge over. That's where to begin. Give your attention to it.

Suppose you are given charge of Winston, the dog. This is your chance to be a man in the making. Use your authority to serve Winston. Faithfully feed him breakfast every day. Provide a warm place for him to sleep. Brush him. Teach him good manners and protect him from mean dogs. You have the power to treat him well or to be mean. The way you use your authority shows the kind of man that you are.

As you grow in strength and authority, I hope you will always use your power to care for the "chickens" in your life and never accidentally shoot them.

...authority, which the Lord hath given us for edification and not for your destruction... (2 Corinthians 10:8).

Questions

• Who or what are the "chickens" in your life? (A chicken is something or someone under your authority.)

• Strength brings authority. What are your areas of strength?

• How can you use your areas of strength to help others?

• Have you ever used your power to hurt others?

• Will you purpose to use your authority to serve people?

From his residence in the castle, Emmanuel observed what was happening in the town. He realized that by the policy of Mr. Carnal Security, the hearts of the men of Mansoul had turned cold in their love for him.

—John Bunyan, *The Holy War*

One Degree at a Time

Do you know how to use a magnetic compass? I hope you do. It is important for a man to know his position and his direction as he travels this world. A simple compass, with a little training and practice, will help you travel confidently. It is useful in the woods or in a busy city. With it, you can provide directions to help others reach their destinations. Knowing which way you want to go can save hours of frustration. If you don't have a compass, get one. Learn how to use it. You will never regret it.

Another great tool is a thermometer. Simple thermometers tell you the temperature inside or outside your house. You can play games guessing the temperature. Then check yourself with a thermometer. In time you will confidently be able to sense the correct temperature. That could be important when you are driving a car. When your senses tell you, "It's freezing out here," you will be alert for icy roads. It just might save your life.

These two simple tools help you to be more aware of what is happening around you. In the Pacific Northwest, if you feel a warm wind coming out of the south, it usually means rain. It's time to get your bike under cover. A cold wind out of the east means that it could freeze tonight. A wise response might be to put a tarp over the tomato plants.

A compass and a thermometer both measure in units called degrees. A compass has 360 degree marks around its edge. A thermometer can have any number of degree marks on it, depending on its size. My yard thermometer records temperatures from -60 to 120 degrees.

Both instruments are usually used to calculate change. They show the direction of the change and the amount of

the change. All changes take place one degree at a time. You can never skip a degree in change.

If you jump in the air and spin completely around before landing, you have traveled 360 degrees. You passed every degree in your jump, though you were fast about it. When water warms from 32 degrees to 100 degrees, it must pass through every degree between 32 and 100. Change occurs one degree at a time.

This is important because YOU are changing. You are changing from a boy to a man. You are changing in body size. Your mind is growing in wisdom and knowledge. Your heart is developing in character. Your spirit is expanding as God's Spirit progressively fills you. All of this is happening one degree at a time. Sometimes you may not notice the change until quite a few degrees have passed. Great-aunt Betty exclaims, "Billy, you have grown a foot since I saw you last!" She might be right but it was little by little, one degree of measurement at a time.

Changing into a man is a continual process. It is learning one line after another, one precept after the next, here a little, there a little. Many boys wait for the big jump of growth. It never comes. A man that is faithful in big things was faithful for years in little things. Diligence is careful, steady effort: today, tomorrow, and the next day. It is not necessarily speedy, but it always arrives at the destination.

If you want to be good at math, don't worry about how big the book is, simply do today's lesson well. If you want to memorize a chapter, don't be overwhelmed by its length. Just work on the one sentence for today. The rest will come in time. All good skills and qualities come little by little, one degree at a time.

Beware—the opposite is also true. All bad qualities develop one degree after another. The slothful man becomes lazy one soft choice after another. He may lie in bed only one minute after his alarm goes off. One minute, that is almost nothing. Tomorrow it may be only one minute more. Slowly, those minutes add up. Two months from now, he may be lying in bed for an hour after his alarm rings. It is only a *little* sleep. It is only a *little* slumber. It is only a *little* folding of the hands to rest. One degree at a time, the once-diligent man becomes a sloth.

A number of years ago I needed to change, but I was just too busy to do so. One degree at a time my heart was growing cold. I could sense it. I did nothing, but God did.

Our family lived on a tree farm in a travel trailer. The thin walls of the trailer allowed us to experience each season of the year. We felt the warmth of summer and the cold of winter.

One particular winter was exceptionally cold. Maintaining running water became a challenge. Throughout the night we kept a trickle of water going in the bathroom sink. I woke regularly, listening for the gurgling sound and then falling back asleep.

The water in the well is about 55 degrees year round. If it keeps running, the pipes cannot freeze. But when the water stops flowing and the temperature is well below freezing, all the lines freeze. If that happens, there is no more water to the trailer until the weather warms, and that could be weeks.

At 2:30 one morning I awoke. The water had stopped! Without hesitation I jumped out of bed. Throwing on warm clothes, I went out into the night. First, I crawled under the trailer and squeezed all the hoses checking for a hard spot that would indicate a frozen blockage. The hoses seemed okay. Then I ran two hundred yards down the hill to the pump house looking for trouble there.

Unable to find any frozen pipes I ran back up to the trailer for a heater…down to the pump house to plug it in…up to the trailer for a lamp to put by the hoses…down to the pump to check for any progress.

I raced back and forth knowing that the longer it took to find the frozen block, the colder all the lines would become.

On one trip up the road I stopped my busyness and looked up into the sky. The stars were brilliant. The night was so cold and calm that I could hear my heart beat. In the stillness God spoke to my spirit:

"When your water lines begin to freeze, you jump out of bed immediately, even in the middle of the night. It is important for you to have drinking water. When the Living Water in your heart begins to freeze, are you that quick to get up and attend to the trouble?"

I had been busy lately. The cares of the world were gradually freezing the water of my heart. Slowly, one degree at a time, I was growing cold toward God and wasn't doing anything about it. I knew the water was slowing, but spiritually I continued to lie in bed. On that freezing night, halfway between the trailer and the pump house, His presence melted my heart, one degree at a time. He showed me again the purpose of life, reminded me of His love, and drew me to His warm side.

It took two hours to find and fix the water line. A short, quarter-inch pipe to the pressure gauge had frozen. A few minutes after setting up a light bulb to warm the pipe we had water. Everyone rejoiced to have running water again, but it mattered little to me compared to having warm Living Water flowing in my heart once more.

Learning to be a man includes learning to calculate the direction and the temperature of your heart. Be willing to change that direction the instant you sense you are one degree off course. When your heart temperature loses one degree of warmth toward God, make changes right away. A small good change today may prevent years of trouble in the future.

***Today if ye will hear his voice,
harden not your hearts*** (Hebrews 4:5).

Questions

- Which way is north?

- What temperature is it in the room?

- Name a tool useful to test the temperature and direction of a man's heart.

- What happens if you are not alert to the changes in your heart?

- Are you growing toward godliness or godlessness?

- Do you want to change or grow in an area of your life? What is one small step you can make in that direction today?

Be Strong!
We are not here to play, to dream, to drift;
We have hard work to do, and loads to lift;
Shun not the struggle—face it; 'tis God's gift.

Be Strong!
Say not, "The days are evil. Who's to blame?"
And fold the hands and acquiesce—oh shame!
Stand up, speak out, and bravely, in God's name.

Be Strong!
It matters not how deep entrenched the wrong,
How hard the battle goes, the day how long;
Faint not—fight on! Tomorrow comes the song.

—Maltbie Davenport Babcock

A Man

Springfield, Oregon 1938

Whiney didn't want to get up, didn't like his breakfast, and didn't want to go to the dentist. He complained about the rain, thought they should have gotten a closer parking place, and almost cried when his mother demanded that he get out of the car and get into the office. Whiney thought the chairs were too hard. He couldn't find a book or magazine to suit him.

It wasn't just because he had to go to the dentist that Whiney made such a fuss. He acted like this every day. It seemed like a rain cloud always hung over his head.

"Whiney," called the dental assistant, announcing that it was his turn to follow her down the hall. He tried to grab his mother's skirt, but she moved out of the way and said sharply, "Follow the lady."

In the chair, Whiney squirmed. Whiney kicked. Whiney refused to do anything Dr. Dow asked.

"Sit up and act like a man," said the dentist.

"I don't want to be a man," whined Whiney.

Dr. Dow could hardly believe his ears! "You don't want to be a man?" To the dentist, being a man was a trophy, a great honor, and the goal of every boy's life. It grieved him to have in his chair a boy who spoke against the very reason and purpose for his own existence. God creates boys to become men.

Of course, Whiney wasn't his real name; it's been changed to protect the guilty. But the dentist, his office, and the incident were real. It is sad to say that many boys today are growing up like Whiney—maybe you know some. And, if you are honest, you might admit that you act like Whiney from time to time.

Nate Miller wrote, "Winter brings the kind of weather you either face head on and enjoy, or shrink from all season long." Being a man is similar. It is not an easy road. At times it's a struggle, a fight. However, the other option is to remain an undeveloped boy. A boy without the courage to be a man shrinks from the cold, from climbing mountains, from fighting battles—and then wonders why life is dull and meaningless.

Being a man is more difficult now than in 1938 when Dr. Dow was a dentist. Many people in our society are against the idea of boys becoming men. When a man makes a definite decision and sticks by it, he is accused of arrogance. If he sets boundaries for those under him, he's overprotective. When he refuses to lower his moral standards, he's labeled old-fashioned. Books, magazines, and movies often make fun of genuine manhood.

The current pursuit of pleasure, leisure, and selfishness stunts the growth of men. Many fathers still live as boys. It may be a difficult era for a boy to learn to be a man. That gives all the more reason to say, "This is the day for me! Let's begin the course. Let's fight the fight! I want to be the man God created me to be!"

Always a great hindrance to a boy becoming a true man is open rebellion against God. Many outspoken individuals attempt to make America Godless. Some foolish people want to remove all references to God from every public area. They promote the lie of evolution and say that people are just animals, alive by chance. However, there can be no fulfillment in living apart from the One who created life. Without an active relationship with God, true manhood is never achieved.

God created the universe so that anyone who looks upon it will know what He is like. When you look at the stars, you see His boundless size. When you watch a spider spinning a web, you see a display of His attention to detail. The invisible things of God are clearly seen in creation. They are a witness to His eternal power and divinity.

God's greatest creation is man. Man is a tent in which God desires to live and display Himself to the world. If you see a mature man filled with God's Spirit, you see the heart of God in what that man does. If you see an immature man without the Spirit of God, you witness the corruption that a selfish creature apart from God can demonstrate.

Young man, you have a high calling and a tremendous purpose ahead of you. The God of the universe wants to show Himself to the world through you. He wants to dwell in you. He wants to use your hands and your feet, your smile, and your words to display Himself to those He brings into your life. The greatest privilege of a man is to display the nature of God. Will you let Him complete this purpose in you? Will you give up your selfishness and embrace a higher calling? Will you trade in your toys and pleasures for a life of purpose, usefulness, and glory?

There is not a set day when you become a man. It's not a matter of age. Manhood is built within you little by little. Each time you accept one of life's responsibilities as your own, you take a step toward manhood. One step could be a decision to wash the car regularly. Even if you do not have a driver's license, you could purpose to keep it clean for the family to enjoy.

Each time you claim some task as your own, you advance toward manhood. When you begin to see the needs of others and feel the urge to meet those needs, you're becoming a man. When you develop a useful skill, gain wisdom, or protect someone that is weak, you are moving toward your life purpose. Every time you act the way God would act toward those around you, you fulfill His hope for you. You are living like a man.

Developing in manhood is a process. It comes with small daily choices. Every time you obey God instead of following a selfish desire, you're growing in manhood. Whenever you give up your comfort to bring comfort to another, you're changing from a boy to a man. Though it is a process, you have the opportunities today to advance toward the goal. You can be more of man today than you were yesterday and farther along tomorrow than today. It's your decision. Regardless of your age, you can still begin to act like a man in the areas you understand.

The lessons ahead of you come from men who have faced life. They have tasted the thrill of victories and the dust of defeats, and by God's grace they have stood up again.

May you see the grand privilege before you of being the man God intends you to be. As old Doctor Dow said, "Sit up and act like a man!"

*So God created man in his own image,
in the image of God created he him; male
and female created he them* (Genesis 1:27).

Questions

- What did Nate Miller write about winter?

- How does winter relate to manhood?

- When does a boy become a man?

- What is the greatest privilege given to man?

*The most manifest sign of wisdom
is a continual cheerfulness.*

—Michel de Montaigne

Be of Good Cheer

One summer, in the early 1970s, Doug Jordan and I hitchhiked from North Carolina to our home in Oregon. We saw many sights and met wonderful folks who helped us on our way. We stopped at a summer camp in the hills outside Nashville, Tennessee. The manager invited us to stay for a week to build outhouses. We accepted the offer and went to work immediately.

For many of the high school students at the camp, this was their first time outside a city. Without streetlights, neon signs, and large buildings to light up the night, it was dark in the woods. If it weren't for the cabin lights and campfires, the total darkness would have overcome those city kids with fear.

The campers slept inside cabins all week except for the last night. Everyone imagined the fun they would have that night singing around a bright crackling campfire. Rumors flew about roasting marshmallows, eating thick tasty stew, and sleeping in a makeshift lean-to. Late in the afternoon on the final day, five different groups loaded their belongings on their backs and hiked to their camping spots.

That evening Doug and I decided to tour each camp. The first campers excitedly offered us some of that tasty stew. There was a buzz of activity: some chopped wood; some arranged supplies; some played. Spirits were high for this grand event. The camps radiated with the light and cheer of a blazing fire. Happy chatter echoed far down the trails.

Where was Camp Five? We knew where it was supposed to be, but we couldn't see any fire, nor hear any chatter. Entering a clearing, we heard faint whimpers and sniffs. Our flashlight beams exposed the faces of twelve scared girls. They huddled together wrapped in blankets. Unable to start a fire, the happy camping night turned into terror. Afraid of snakes, no one wanted to go for help. Their only action was to cry.

Doug scrounged up some paper and kindling. He took a match from his pocket and struck it on a rock. Just the light of a match seemed to bring hope. Within minutes his cheery fire changed the atmosphere. Tears dried. Sighs relieved the tension. One girl straightened up the bedding. Another got out some food. First, we heard a little humming, then a stanza, and soon everyone joined in a lively camp song.

A crackling fire changed gloom and despair into hope, laughter, and the smell of stew.

Leaving the happy group, Doug called back, "The angel of the Lord encampeth round them that fear Him and delivereth them." During the night, whenever anyone became fearful, they reviewed that verse. The reminder of a guarding angel brought cheerful confidence. The next morning, Camp Five presented us with a rock on which they had inscribed the verse Doug had quoted, Psalm 34:7.

For many people, the world is a dark, fearful place. They feel that evil is in control, or that life happens by chance. Many wander without purpose, afraid that the worst is just about to happen. Some people live in gloom because they are selfish. They pout because they can't have ice cream after dinner or because they can't sit in the front seat of the car. Discontented people live in self-made darkness.

God provides enough light in our world to keep every creature confident, hopeful, and bright. He takes pleasure in starting cheerful fires, even for those who reject that light. Sin made the world as dark as a fireless campsite on a cloudy night. God sent His Son, the Light of the world, to bring hope to men who have lost their courage. He brings truth to those overcome with lies. His presence brings light so that men could see the meaning and purpose for life.

Look at these examples of how Jesus brought light to everyday experiences. "Cheer up," Jesus said to the lame man as his friends lowered him on a stretcher through the roof. "Cheer up, your sins are forgiven."

To the disciples rowing against the wind, who screamed thinking a ghost came to get them, "Cheer up, it is Me!" was His happy reply.

Paul sat in a dark jail wondering about his life's direction. The Lord appeared and said, "Be of good cheer, Paul…thou…must bear witness also at Rome."

When Jesus told His disciples of His coming death, they became fearful. He encouraged them saying, "Cheer up. I have overcome the world." Jesus brought light to His world. With that light came courage, confidence, and hope.

God still brings His light into everyday life. He desires people to confidently face any trouble by the light of His truth. He would like to use you to spread that light. Your purpose in life is to display the heart of our cheerful God to your world. You have the privilege of bringing joy, hope, and cheery light to all you meet, because God has first given it to you. Here are two practical examples of how to do it.

Stopping to visit a friend named Gabe, you find him discouraged. He is staring at a math book.

"I'm such a dummy," he laments. "I forgot the formula for how to find the area of a circle. I know that it has 'R's and 'Pi's in it, but I just can't remember how they go. I will never become an engineer if I can't remember a simple formula."

Here is your chance to bring light and cheerfulness to him. Speaking the truth you say, "Gabe, you are not a dummy; you just don't remember the formula. I don't remember it either, but that dictionary over there does." You grab the dictionary and thumb to the charts in the back. "Here it is! It's πr^2. If you multiply the radius of the circle times itself and then multiply that times π (and π equals approximately 3.14) you get the area of a circle." You continue to speak the truth, "Gabe, any boy willing to diligently work at it is able to be an engineer. Don't worry. With careful effort, you won't fail!"

On the street you meet Becky. She looks sad. "Something got you down today, Beck?" you ask.

"Oh yes," is her reply. "Dad is sick and he can't work. If he doesn't get better, we won't be able to pay the rent. Then we will have to move. Where will we go?" Becky's imagination is overflowing with fear and darkness. How can you shine light into her imagination?

Again, you speak the truth.

"Becky, now is the time to see God's provision, first-hand. He likes providing for wives and children when dads are sick. Keep alert and you will see His work. Get a notebook. Write down every time your family receives some provision that you didn't expect. Thank God for this opportunity! Cheer up and you will see Him."

If you have any means to help her, you could offer her even a small amount of money. Tell her to use it if times get tough. In the meanwhile, she could set that money in a visible spot as a reminder that God will provide.

A cheerful boy is a light shining in a dark world. Every day he tells the world, "Good is coming if you will receive it!" He spreads light by speaking truth to those hearing lies. He has hope because he believes the Bible when it says that all things work together for good to those who love God. He has courage to live because he knows that his God is in control of his future. He has every reason to rejoice and no reason to despair. You can be that boy.

Get to know the truth. Refuse to let yourself become discouraged. Let God's cheerful Spirit rule your heart. Life is full of hope. If you find yourself sliding into discouragement or into a sour attitude, know for sure that you are listening to some form of a lie. Go back to the truth and believe it. God always gives enough light to brighten your own heart— with plenty of extra to spill over into lives around you.

If you will let cheerfulness dwell in your heart, you will brighten the lives of many fearful and hurting people, just like Doug did for those terrified girls.

...for the joy of the Lord is your strength
(Nehemiah 8:10).

Questions

- Why does darkness bring fear?

- What truth did Doug give that provided light and hope all night long?

- What is an example of a match that you can use to light a dark life?

- What "fire" could you start for a lonely person? A sick person?

- How do you keep your own heart cheerful?

When, therefore, the first spark of a desire after God arises in thy soul, cherish it with all thy care, give all thy heart into it; it is nothing less than a touch of the divine Loadstone that is to draw thee out of the vanity of time into the riches of eternity.

—William Law, *The Spirit of Prayer*

Coveting

"Hey! Look at the wallpaper I got!"

"There's enough paint here to cover my whole house!"

"I've gathered so much that I'm going to have a garage sale this weekend and make a fortune!"

These were some of the comments I heard from the men working on the new Willamette Oaks retirement center in Eugene, Oregon. My job was installing woodwork in the common areas, staircases, and front entry. As workers walked by with armloads of building materials, they often made these comments about their plunder. The attitude escalated until it felt like the goal each day was to collect materials, rather than complete the building.

I was preparing to build a house for my family. I also faced the temptation to take the wood that I assumed the company didn't want. I could feel my heart change from desiring solely to be a good worker to the double mind of serving the boss but wanting wood for myself.

One particular morning I wrestled with my desires. As I walked across the parking lot, I put an end to the struggle by quietly praying, "Lord, I don't want to have a covetous heart. I want a heart that concentrates on giving my boss a full day's work. Let the scraps be his scraps, not mine. If You want me to have anything from this job, You make the company force it on me." With a single mind I returned to work, feeling light and free.

Leroy, the job superintendent, came looking for me. He found me on the fourth floor, trimming the windows of a meeting room. "You're getting ready to build a house aren't you?" he asked.

"Yes, I am."

"Well then, everything on the north side of the building is yours," he declared as he walked out of the room.

During the lunch break I walked around to the north side. Piles of lumber, laminated beams, insulation, and plywood filled the storage area. The home base for this company was in Spokane, Washington. It was cheaper for them to dispose of the extra material than to haul it from the middle of Oregon to the eastern edge of Washington, five hundred miles away.

I walked back into the building, found Leroy, and asked him, "What did you mean that everything on the north side of the building was mine? There is a lot of wood out there."

"Yes, and it is all yours," he said.

I went back to the fourth floor. In the middle of tools, lumber, and sawdust I knelt and prayed again. "Thank You, Lord, for freeing my heart from coveting and for giving me more materials than I imagined."

There was more lumber out there than I could stack on two commercial lumber trucks. How would I haul it away? As I thought about it, a friend of mine who also worked on the project stepped into my room. He asked if he could have some four-by-fours. "Why are you asking me?" I questioned.

"Leroy said that everything out there was yours," he replied.

I told him to take what he needed. That began a steady stream of men requesting this or that.

When the landscaper's helper asked for a piece of plywood to patch his pump house, I inquired, "What's left?"

"That is about it," he answered.

"If you clean up everything, you can have it," I told him.

I didn't receive one stick of lumber from those piles. What I did receive was freedom in my heart to work without the desire to take wood for myself. I acquired an inner contentment and an awareness of God's presence, which is worth more than an entire lumberyard. With His presence came the confidence that whenever I needed anything, He would provide it.

God knew my future. I didn't. If I had taken that material, it would have been a burden to me. I didn't know then that we were about to move to the town of Cheshire. I would have had to haul it there from our house in Springfield. Later, we moved up the McKenzie River to the place where we eventually built a house. I would have had to move that wood three times before using it.

Instead of hauling that lumber around, God got rid of it for me. When it came time to build our house, guess what company came back to town and wanted me to work for them? You're right, and Leroy was in charge.

At the end of the job he wanted me to haul off the extra trim lumber. There was so much that I could hardly fit it on the lumber rack of my truck. Some boards were worth a hundred dollars each! They were so valuable that I called the owner of the company to be sure I wasn't doing something illegal. He got a little angry that I would interrupt his day and said, "If Leroy tells you to take it, take it and don't bother me!" *Click,* he hung up the phone.

God knows what we need and what we don't need. He knows when to give it and when to take it away. Sometimes we reflect God's glory by having things. Sometimes we reflect Him best when we don't have anything at all. As a Christian man matures, he learns to be content with little and with much—whichever God gives to him that day.

One of God's Ten Commandments is, "Thou shalt not covet." Coveting is the desire to obtain and possess something that doesn't belong to you. God gives this commandment not because He doesn't want you to have anything, but because coveting will keep you from possessing what you need and want most.

When a man covets, he is unable to enjoy the presence of God. Foremost in his mind is the item he wants. He dreams about it. He schemes about how to get it. He becomes so full of his desire that his heart has no room to experience God's presence. The man has lost his trust in God to supply his need. His focus, his attention, is getting the item he wants. Sometimes he will resort to whining, to deception, and even to outright theft. That is why the Bible says that covetousness is idolatry. It is having something in our hearts that holds more of our attention and desire than God holds.

Mr. Toolson told me of the time when, as a boy, he worked at a store. Hungry, he ate a candy bar, fully intending to pay for it before he left for the day. He forgot and went home without paying for the candy. When he remembered his mistake, he immediately returned to the job to pay his boss. The boss was extremely pleased. Mr. Toolson went home knowing that he had a job for life if he wanted it. And, what was more, he had a clear conscience.

What would you rather have, a "free" candy bar or a clear conscience and the respect of your boss?

If something doesn't belong to you, don't covet it and don't possess it. If you find an item that was lost or stolen, locate the owner and return it. The usefulness and happiness of a man does not depend upon what he acquires. Fullness of joy depends upon the awareness of God's presence. Anything that threatens that awareness is not worth having.

Whenever you begin to covet, when you take or keep what doesn't belong to you, remember that you are about to lose something of great worth. You will lose a clear conscience. You will lose the privilege of watching a supernatural God miraculously provide for you. But most of all, you will lose the joy God offers to those who desire Him above all else.

...be without covetousness; and be content with such things as ye have: for he hath said, I will never leave thee, nor forsake thee (Hebrews 13:5).

Questions

- What does it mean to covet?

- Why is coveting considered idolatry?

- What do you lose when you covet?

- What is it that allows a man to live with contentment and joy?

Idle men tempt the devil to tempt them.

—Charles H. Spurgeon

Temptation

You receive an invitation in the mail. Someone desires your presence at an important event! It's a birthday party. Maybe it's a wedding. Better yet, how about a camping trip? The reason somebody sends you an invitation is because they want you to be there. Usually the envelopes are carefully addressed and attractive. The purpose of an invitation is to provide you with all the information you need so you can come to the right place at the right time. It gives you the details in a style that will make you want to come.

Temptations are invitations to do evil. Everyone receives them. Each temptation invites you to destroy your life. Every invitation to do evil, no matter how small, is designed to destroy some valuable part of you. Temptations look good, but they always contain a lie. They don't tell *all* the truth.

Suppose that you are walking down the alley after dark. An evil invitation comes to you through a thought or maybe from a boy walking beside you. Though it may be words or thoughts, the invitation is as clear as if it were written on fine paper:

There's old man Benson's garage.
He kept our baseball when it rolled into his yard
     last week.
Let's throw a rock and break out a window.
Benson is mean.
He deserves a broken window.
Nobody will see us.
He is gone for the night.
This will be fun!

There is the invitation calling you to join the party. The trouble is that these invitations lie. If it were possible to turn over the invitation and see the truth written on the back, you would find something like this:

You are cordially invited to throw a rock at Mr.
     Benson's window.
Remember, God is watching you.
Is it kind to break windows?
You will feel guilty all of your life, even if you don't
     get caught.
If you do get caught, you will have to pay the dam-
     ages with your savings.
You will lose your good name, your parents' confi-
     dence, and the job Mr. Jones was about to offer
     you.
Not only will you be called a vandal, you will be one.
Mr. Benson isn't home tonight because his wife is in
     the hospital.
Do you want to add more pain to his difficult day?

There is the truth of the invitation. Does breaking a window sound like much fun now? If you accept even a small invitation to do evil, you damage your life and destroy good opportunities that were coming your way.

If you find that you enjoy yielding to invitations, you are in more danger than you know. Many small temptations entice you into poor habits of life. The more invitations that you accept, the more you will receive. Every time you yield to temptation, you are the loser.

How can a boy who wants to do well avoid falling to temptations? Overcoming evil is not a matter of fighting. Evil is overcome by doing good. When good invitations arrive at your life's door, accept as many as possible. It's easier to say no to evil temptations when you're busy with good opportunities. Attending to your work and study will interfere with many tempting events.

In the middle of well doing and attending to your responsibilities, temptations will still present themselves. They will invite you to give yourself to something selfish, sensual, or evil. Every temptation you face is common to other boys. God has seen it before, and He is on your side. He has already planned a way of escape and wants to tell you about it.

Therefore, the secret to overcoming temptations is to ask this question, "God, what should I be doing now?" If you ask with a heart ready to obey, the way of escape will always appear. The reply might be, "You are supposed to be helping your dad work on the car." If that is the case, go help him. Maybe you will hear, "You said that you would deliver papers with Roger." Get going, catch up to him.

When you know the path of escape, take it! It is a gift to you from God. Don't try to fight temptations; ask and obey. Overcome the invitation to do evil with God's invitation to do good.

Here is an example. Mom said, "Don't eat any cake." You stand looking at it, drooling on your shirt and imagining how tasty it must be. You're sure that no one will notice if you take just one small bite. The struggle rages inside. You don't want to take it…you do want to take it…you don't want to take it…

This is the time to ask, "God, what should I be doing right now?" He will always give you a way of escape. Maybe He will say, "Go brush your teeth." Obey His voice and the temptation is over.

Many men go through life struggling and fighting with one temptation after another. They try to stand strong against evil desires but continually lose. They don't want to fall but just don't have the strength to win. Overcoming does not come by being tough and strong. It comes by simply following what God says to do.

Jehoshaphat, an Old Testament king of Israel, gives us a great example of how to overcome an enemy attack. It is also the way to overcome temptation. When Moab and Ammon came to fight against Israel, Jehoshaphat prayed to God, "…we have no might against this great company that cometh against us; neither know we what to do: but our eyes are upon thee."

God responds through a prophet, "Be not afraid nor dismayed by reason of this great multitude; for the battle is not yours, but God's…ye shall not need to fight in this battle: set yourselves, stand ye still, and see the salvation of the Lord with you, O Judah and Jerusalem: fear not, nor be dismayed; tomorrow go out against them: for the Lord will be with you" (2 Chronicles 20).

Jehoshaphat went out the next day just like God said. The Israelites didn't go out to fight but sent out singers in the front ranks to face the enemy. When they reached Moab and Ammon, they found all of them dead. The enemies had fought among themselves and killed each other.

Israel spent the next three days picking up the rich spoils that the armies left scattered on the battlefield.

When you are faced with temptations, when a battle seems to be looming in front of you, ask God, "What do I do now?" and obey what He tells you. He's prepared a path for your escape. Follow it. You'll be free; He'll be honored.

> *There hath no temptation taken you but such as is common to man: but God is faithful, who will not suffer you to be tempted above that ye are able; but will with the temptation also make a way to escape, that ye may be able to bear it* (1 Corinthians 10:13).

Questions

- What invitations to do evil did you get today? Did you take any?

- If you accept an evil invitation, what will happen to you?

- When faced with a temptation, what question should you ask?

- Did you accept any invitations to do good today?

Education comprehends all that series of instruction and discipline which is intended to enlighten the understanding, correct the temper, and form the manners and habits of youth, and fit them for usefulness in their future stations.

—Noah Webster

Education for Life

Rodney wanted to hunt turkeys. Ten years ago, a pair of wild turkeys were introduced into the valley. They multiplied and began taking over the family farm! It was time to think about controlling their numbers and eating a fresh turkey for Thanksgiving.

Before Rodney could hunt turkeys, he needed a hunting license. Before he could get a hunting license, the law required that he pass a hunters' safety course.

The safety course teaches young hunters to be responsible with guns, respectful of other people's property, and resourceful with the harvested animals. Rodney signed up for the class. Each Tuesday and Thursday evening for four weeks he met with other hunting students.

On Saturday of the last week, he attended the all-day field class. There the young hunters practiced handling guns safely in real-life situations, like getting in and out of a truck or climbing over a fence. Using BB guns and cardboard targets, the instructors taught them how to shoot from various positions. On their bellies, sitting, standing, and kneeling, they practiced safety and accuracy. The highlight of the day was shooting clay pigeons with real shotguns. The safety course and the lessons his father had already taught him gave Rodney confidence that he could hunt safely.

Early one cold November day, Rodney quietly waited behind an old oak tree. *Gobble-gobble.* A flock of turkeys cautiously filed up the trail. Whenever he got excited, Rodney had the tendency to talk quietly to himself. He began whispering the lessons he had learned, "Yep, those are legal turkeys. If I overshoot, the bank behind them will stop the shot. Remove your safety. Pull the trigger slow…and…eeeeeasy."

Then his gun spoke up. *BOOM!* The lead turkey dropped in his tracks. Rodney calmly stood and slowly

walked to the bird. His dad, who watched from a few yards back, joined him with a pat on the shoulder.

"Great shot, son! Mom will turn him into a fine Thanksgiving dinner."

Education is the act of gaining knowledge and skills to use in a future situation. Rodney wanted a turkey. He received an education from experiences with his father and from the hunters' safety class that fit him for the occasion. In the right season, he put his education into practice and brought home a turkey.

A soldier receives an education in fighting before he is sent into battle. A lifeguard is educated about saving people from drowning before being hired at the pool. Two basic questions should be asked before beginning an educational course. One, what situations will I face in the future? And two, how can I best fit myself for those situations? The answers to those questions help give direction for a useful education.

The life of an educated man is easy compared to the uneducated man. The man with an education is prepared. He has the skills to avoid trouble, to fix problems, and chart new courses. An uneducated man is never quite ready for what happens to him. He doesn't know what to do and misses opportunities because he wasn't prepared.

The last situation that you need to be prepared for is the Judgment throne of God. Every man will one day die, and then face that Judgment. The greatest education available to any man allows him to walk with Jesus Christ past the Judgment, into eternal life. If your education did not include preparation for this event, it was a worthless education—no matter where you got it or how much you paid for it.

Many other important future situations are waiting for you. Will you be ready to take on the role of a caring husband, a useful father, a leader in your community and church, a provider and protector? You might say, "I am only fourteen years old. Why should I think about getting married or about the end of life?" Because it's best to be ready *before* the time comes.

Many men live one step behind life's events. They try to learn to work after they get a job. They seek a class for husbands after they are struggling in their marriage. They read about fatherhood after their children rebel. A good education prepares a young man for his future situations *before* they come.

Education and going to school are not necessarily the same thing. You may attend the best college, graduate with highest honors, and still remain uneducated. Even if you have a degree, you are uneducated if you are not ready for the coming events in your life. The American educational system expects each student to spend about sixteen years becoming "educated" to get a successful job. Earning money and job security are often the goals. When students get their college degrees they are told, and often think, they are educated. They may be fit for a job; however, if they remain unfit for the majority of life's situations they remain uneducated. Life is much more than having a job.

There may be times to enroll in classes to learn useful skills. But it is a fool who spends most of his preparation years learning to earn money if in the process he develops habits and perspectives that make him unfit for godly living. Countless young men who say that they believe in God go off to school to prepare for a good job. Many return with diplomas, yet stripped of their faith. An education that fits a man for a small area of his life and in the process makes him unfit for life's greatest events is a poor education.

"All scripture is given by inspiration of God, and is profitable for doctrine, for reproof, for correction, for instruction in righteousness: that the man of God may be perfect, thoroughly furnished unto all good works" (2 Timothy 3:16). The Scriptures were given that a man could be fit for every situation to come. It's not that the Bible will teach you how to plumb a house or fly an airplane. It teaches you God's perspective on life, His perspective on you. With that viewpoint, when you grow in knowledge of life skills you will know how to think rightly about your skills and how to use them for good. God's perspective is the basis of a good education because He understands how life works.

The Bible is the framework for all knowledge. The man who submits his education and knowledge to the ways of the Bible is the man prepared for the future. Whether he is hunting turkeys or standing before the great Judgment seat, he'll be ready for both.

That's a good education.

Prepare to meet thy God... (Amos 4:12).

Questions

- What is education?

- What did Rodney want to do? How did he get his education?

- What do you want to be educated for?

- What are you doing to be educated?

- What is the most important situation you will ever face? Are you prepared for it?

*He that cannot forgive others breaks
the bridge over which he must pass
himself; for every man has need to be
forgiven.*

—Thomas Fuller

Forgiveness and Dirty Diapers

The Old Man collected dirty diapers—not clean diapers, dirty diapers. Some were antique; some, fresh. They came in all sizes and smells. He knew the contents of each one. His favorite diapers filled a backpack that he wore everywhere he went. He kept these especially close to him for continual review. The not-so-favorite ones he brought out occasionally, and lined them up on the counter. Looking at the array, he remembered the time he collected each one. He could almost give the date, the hour, and the place where he found each soiled rag. The newest diapers were all disposable, but to him, they were keepers. He couldn't, or wouldn't, throw any away. The Old Man spent many happy hours…well, you couldn't call them *happy* hours…yet, he found some strange enjoyment in reviewing his collection.

When he met someone from his past, he would rummage through his pack. Next, he pawed through his pile on the table. Finally, if need be, he tunneled into his storehouse in the garage until he found one of their old diapers. Sometimes he put it right up to their face for a good look and a not-so-good smell. The previous owners usually didn't even recognize it. But the Old Man knew whose it was. His memory failed him on many occasions, but never when it came to the source and description of his diapers. Even after sixty years he could describe them as if he had obtained them yesterday. His collection was impressive for its completeness. You could mention almost anyone alive, and he had one that once belonged to them.

The Old Man, his house, his clothes, and his car all smelled alike. Some folks could manage to endure a few minutes with him. Most avoided even a casual conversation. He grew lonely. In his loneliness, the diaper collection became more valuable than ever.

Does this man seem strange to you? He should. But don't be too hard on him. You may have a secret diaper collection of your own.

Parents use diapers for babies that do not control themselves. They desire a clean and pleasant removal of a distasteful product. The purpose is to remove the offensive material quickly.

Many people have little control of themselves when it comes to foolish thoughts, words, and actions. People without self-control speak sharply to you. They steal your property. They lie to you. They come into your life, offend you, and then walk out. They leave behind a mess, just like a dirty diaper. What do you do when that happens? Do you save their offense to think about in the future? Or do you take their offense and throw it as far as you can?

The word "forgive" means to send it away from you. If you take the wrong that someone does to you and throw it away, you have forgiven them. You don't throw away the person who wronged you. You throw away the offense. And you throw it far enough to be out of your life and out of theirs.

Today, people get things mixed up. They throw people out of their lives and save the offense—just like the Old Man saving diapers. They have nothing to do with the offender, but they save the offense for their diaper collection.

A young man who continually rehearses the offenses of others becomes bitter. He holds grudges. He is not free to smile at his offenders. He is weighed down by a pack of dirty diapers. He stinks. He cannot enjoy life. He cannot enjoy others and they cannot enjoy him. Every minute that he thinks about the crimes done against him is one minute he is unable to think good thoughts. He wastes his life, re-arranging and reviewing dirty diapers. The clutter in this boy's mind will continually hinder his achievement.

A useful boy cannot waste valuable time thinking about how others have hurt him. He needs a fresh, clear, creative mind. He needs a positive outlook that can see past the puny things others do. This boy has a light step. He is free to think and to do good.

God values a forgiving heart. He has said that if you will not forgive those who wrong you, He will not forgive you. He will put in your face all the dirty diapers you have given to others, if you will not throw away the ones they have given you. That ought to make everyone desire to quickly forgive!

This illustration about the dirty diapers is somewhat crude. But sin is extremely foul, and an unforgiving heart is just as bad. To find pleasure in collecting the faults of others and to find pleasure in remembering them is wrong.

Before we leave this topic, there is one more thing for a growing boy to consider. There are times that you will be offensive to someone else. You will make a mistake or maybe purposefully hurt someone. You can help people you wrong to forgive you by going to them as soon as you are aware of it. Tell them you were wrong. Express your sorrow and ask them to throw away your offense. Give them your word that you won't do it again. A mature man makes right his own wrong—immediately.

For if ye forgive men their trespasses,
your heavenly Father will also forgive you:
But if ye forgive not men their trespasses,
neither will your Father forgive your
trespasses (Matthew 6:14,15).

Questions

- Has anyone ever wronged you?

- Are you still holding onto their "diaper"?

- How do you put a "diaper" in the garbage?

- What does it mean to forgive?

- How can you help others to forgive you?

- What happens if you do not forgive others?

It is very well to tell me that a young man has distinguished himself by a brilliant first speech. He may go on, or he may be satisfied with his first triumph; but show me a young man who has not succeeded at first, and nevertheless has gone on, and I will back that young man to do better than most of those who have succeeded at the first trial.

—Charles James Fox

Get Up Again

On the first play of the season opener, Randy excitedly lined up in the halfback position behind the quarterback. "Hike!" The quarterback took the ball and handed it to Randy. The whole team swept to the right. Behind the blockers he made five yards, and then he broke out into the open along the sidelines. The fans screamed with delight as he ran for the goal! A fast defender shot across the field and knocked Randy flat. What a hit! Randy got up slowly, limped to the bench, and said, "Coach, I quit."

"What do you mean, you quit?" barked the coach. "You are the best runner we have! That last play proves it! You gained sixty-five yards on our first run and now you want to quit! Why?"

"I'm quitting because I got tackled!" whined Randy. "I don't want to be a disgrace to the team, or to myself for that matter. I quit!"

What would you think about a football player who quit the first time he was tackled? Getting tackled is part of the game. No one with the ball wants to be tackled, and certainly no one falls down without a reason. The goal is to score. But getting tackled is the common reality.

Even guys that are not carrying the ball are frequently knocked down. They get blocked, pushed, and sometimes trip themselves. For a player to complain and quit because he was tackled is crazy. Falling to the ground is part of football.

In the game of life, men get tackled, trip, and fall. There is not a man alive who has stayed on his feet throughout life. All have fallen, all have made mistakes, and all have done things that were wrong. Only the foolish will say, "I quit!" The successful quickly jump up and cry, "Give me another chance!"

No man wants to fall and no one tries to fall. Still, all men fall. The difference between men is what they do after they are down. Some try to hide it, afraid that others will think less of them. Some men give up and lie there. The courageous lift up their heads, admit it, make it right, and keep going.

My friend Willie Hansen regularly visits the Eugene Gospel Rescue Mission. The men living there usually have gone through deep troubles. Sometimes people say that they are down and out. Willie says that those guys are no different from you or me except that when most of them fell, they didn't get up promptly. If you won't get up quickly, your troubles will increase.

Suppose your dad says that you can't go to the neighbors until the yard is mowed. He asked you to do it two days ago, but you put it off. Now he is a little upset and speaks sharply to you. You get mad and stomp out of the house. Shock! Do Christian boys ever act like that? Yes. Should they? No. Well, what do you do now that you have? How do you get up?

Here are four courses of action. Which one will get you up the fastest?

A. Justify yourself. Say it is Dad's fault because he shouldn't expect so much and he shouldn't speak sharply.
B. Angrily mow the grass. When it is time for dinner, sit at the table without talking to your dad. Keep up the silent treatment until tomorrow.
C. Admit you fell short. Come back into the house. Humbly apologize to your dad for not mowing the grass sooner, for getting angry, and for stomping out of the house. Ask him to forgive you. Then cheerfully mow the lawn.
D. Just go to the neighbors and forget about it.

If you chose D, "Just go to the neighbors and forget about it," will the situation get better or worse? Once your dad finds out, I think life will suddenly get worse. And it should, because that is not the way to respond when you fail. The way to respond is to get up, and only choice C will get you up quickly. Go back and make it right. If you develop the habit of staying down when you fall, your troubles will increase.

Men who refuse to get up quickly when they fall ruin many relationships. Marriages fail. Folks lose trust in them. The man even dislikes himself. The life of the man who refuses to get up when he falls becomes like an automobile junkyard. All around him lie damaged relationships, dreams smashed like old windshields, dented fenders of the mistakes he won't take the time to pound out. All of these are reminders of his unwillingness to make the effort to get up.

The film *Chariots of Fire* shows the true story of Olympic runner Eric Liddell. In one particular race, the other runners boxed Eric in and tripped him. Down he went. A runner cannot afford to spend much time lying on his back if he ever hopes to win a race. Eric jumped to his feet, well behind all other runners. With an amazing burst of energy Eric not only caught up with the pack, but went ahead to win the race.

If Eric had simply won the race, the fans would have thought well of him. But when he fell, got up, and still won, he became a hero! What courage! What determination! What a man! Eric's example of getting up quickly is the attitude every boy should develop early in his life. Admit your faults, confess your mistakes, and make right your wrongs. As much as is possible, get up and keep running!

It is usually easier to do something well the first time than to redo it after failure. When Nehemiah, an Old Testament prophet, returned to rebuild the walls of Jerusalem, he found a pile of rocks and mortar where the walls once stood. The people complained, "…there is so much rubbish; so that we are not able to build the wall." They wished that they could start fresh with a new wall. But that was not the case; they had to work with what they had, and Nehemiah skillfully encouraged them to brace up their minds and do it.

It is easier to have a friendly relationship with someone you like than to repair a friendship that you have damaged. It is easier to paint a new fence than to repaint one when the paint is peeling off. Your life will not always be on the easiest path; don't expect it to be easy. When your mistakes have made your way more difficult, don't fight it. Set your mind and accomplish the work ahead of you. Don't ever avoid repairing what you have damaged just because it will be hard.

I know a carpenter who broke four joints on the handrail he was installing. He could have been discouraged and thrown it all away, but he decided that this was the opportunity to learn how to repair broken handrail joints. He tried four different methods of repair, one on each joint. Now he knows which method works the best. Responding rightly to his failure gave him wisdom and confidence to fix future mistakes.

God anticipates our falls, and He plans for our recoveries. Failures don't shock Him. He doesn't give up on a man when he falls, and neither should we. The first two chapters of the Bible describe the creation of the world and the creation of man. The third chapter is man's fall. The rest of the book is instruction on how to get up again.

Whenever you fail, never lie down and quit. Get up! Restore. Get up! Reconcile. Get up! Rebuild. Pick up the ball and run. As long as there is even one second on the clock of life, GET UP!

Rejoice not against me, O mine enemy:
when I fall, I shall arise... (Micah 7:8).

Questions

- Why was Randy foolish?

- What happens if you don't get up quickly?

- Why do men try to hide their mistakes?

- What usually happens when you confess your faults?

- How can failure be useful?

The world is not my home, I'm just a passin' through...

—Anonymous

Where Do I Belong?

Dad, I just don't have any friends," began Danny. "I have my brother and little sisters, but there aren't any boys my age around here. We see a few boys occasionally; still I wish I had somebody that I could call a good friend. It seems that I'm just different than the boys in the neighborhood. Some go to public school and others go to private school. Most don't like the things I like. I feel alone. Even when we go to church I feel alone. Dad, I can tell that they think I am strange. Why does our family always seem separate? Sometimes it would be great to just fit in with everybody. I wonder what it would be like to not care about how we live, to just do what everybody else does. Then, would I have friends?"

"Danny," returned Father, "what you are experiencing is a very common feeling. I felt like that when I was your age. To tell you the truth, I often feel like that now. Son, if you are going to live a genuine Christian life, you will spend much time feeling alone. That will be particularly true if you read your Bible and do what it says. You will not fit in with this world.

"Do you remember when the Russian boy, Ivan, visited us?" asked Father.

"I sure do," returned Danny. "He was different. I could hardly understand him. He thought our food tasted too sweet. The weather was too hot for him. I liked him all right, but he was a little peculiar. I guess you would call him a foreigner."

"You are right, Danny, he was a foreigner," said Father. "We enjoyed having him in our home. He was a pleasant boy, but different from us. Wherever we went, everyone we met could instantly tell that he was not from around here. Ivan didn't like being different. But that is just the way it is when you are a foreigner.

"In the Bible, Peter wrote a letter to encourage a particular group of folks. These people were Jews that had become Christians. The struggles they faced are similar to the ones you are facing today.

"Being a Jew was more than just going to the synagogue on the Sabbath day. It meant a lifelong commitment to a particular standard of family, community, and national behavior. You did what the community did, or you were rejected. You believed the same. You ate the same. You celebrated the same. To be different was not acceptable.

"The Jews waited for the Messiah. When Jesus came, some of the common Jews believed that He was the Messiah. Most of the leaders did not. They said that anyone who believed in Jesus would be expelled from the synagogue. That meant being removed from the community.

"Some of these Jewish Christians were killed. Many ran from Jerusalem to seek safety in other parts of the world. These were the people Peter attempted to encourage.

"Consider what these 'strangers' experienced. Their whole past 'church life' came to an end. Those still in the Jewish traditions saw them as heretics led astray by Jesus. Their extended families didn't understand them. Everything in their past seemed like an empty shadow compared to the new life in Christ. However, they couldn't communicate this difference without the established group taking offense and saying things like, 'We used to be good enough for you. Now, you think that you are better than us. You think you know more. Where did you get to be so spiritual?' These believers in Christ no longer belonged.

"Besides being strangers to their own people, they now lived in foreign lands. Their neighbors were suspicious of them and laughed at their clothes and their accents. They were made fun of for their customs and the peculiar way that they fixed their food. The Jewish Christians held tight to their convictions and wouldn't do some of the things that the citizens of the country did. Again they were accused of pride and thinking that they were better than everyone else. There was no place in this world where they could go to belong.

"Peter wrote to people who did not fit anywhere in this world. He told them that they might as well get used to the idea. They will always be outsiders until they reach their home in heaven. That is their country. Here, they will talk like a foreigner, come to different conclusions, raise their children contrary to the norm, work differently, maybe eat differently, dress contrary to the current fashions; they will just be odd. They might be trustworthy people, but others tend to back away from them with a certain amount of suspicion, because they are different.

"Danny, it's the same for you and me. Heaven is our country. We want to live to fit that culture. Don't worry about fitting in with this world. Jesus said that He was going to prepare a place for us. In the meantime, He would like to prepare *us* for that place. If we live as He says to live, we will be ready for the country to come. What would you rather do, Danny? Would you like to fit in with a world that only lasts a few short years? Or would you rather live like a stranger here and learn to fit in for eternity? Keep the right perspective, son, and this world will be a grand adventure. But, it won't be your home. You won't fit in. And in the end you will be glad.

"That feeling you have, to belong somewhere, is a God-given feeling. He wants us to long for His country, where all godly people fit in. Don't waste your feelings longing for oneness here. Save them for that place above all places where you will be one with the Creator of the universe."

"That makes sense, Dad. I know that becoming a man means standing alone. I don't like being alone, and it has been bothering me lately. But today, I'm purposing to do what I know is right, even if it means feeling like a misfit."

"I'm glad to hear it, Danny. If you live what you are saying, you are well on your way to being a man fit for eternity."

But now they desire a better country, that is, an heavenly: wherefore God is not ashamed to be called their God: for he has prepared for them a city (Hebrews 11:16).

Questions

• What did Danny feel like?

• Have you ever felt like Danny?

• Why do Christians not fit in with the world?

- What do you do when it is other Christians that you do not seem to fit in with?

- What can you do now to be sure that you are prepared for heaven when the time comes to go there?

Our England is a garden,
  and such gardens are not made
By singing "Oh, how beautiful"
  and sitting in the shade.

—Rudyard Kipling

Mr. Industry vs. Mr. Sloth

Inside every man is the desire to accomplish great works. Inside every man is the desire to lie around doing nothing. Every day both of these desires will draw you. The desire you follow will determine the man you become. Here is a true story of one man named Howard and his mental fight to accomplish a goal. Howard tells the story in his own words.

My garden is a group of raised beds separated by small walkways. Every two years, I add a fresh layer of wood chips to the walks to keep my boots out of the mud.

My two years had expired. A mound of chips waited patiently just off the driveway. I needed someone to move them from the pile to the paths.

At times I am industrious, working like a beaver, finishing project after project. At other times I am slothful, postponing my work. Even when I am feeling industrious, my mind is frequently interrupted by slothful thoughts. I've come to attach names to the thoughts in my mind that encourage me to work.

I call those thoughts Mr. Industry. The thoughts that encourage me to do little or nothing, I call Mr. Sloth.

A few days ago I had been enjoying Mr. Sloth's advice. It was raining outside. I sat in the house. During the time that I should have been spreading chips, I comfortably read a book. The prodding of Mr. Industry would not let me enjoy the story. He often disturbs me when I am listening to Mr. Sloth. Today was no exception. Industry paced back and forth making statements like, "Put out the chips and then read your book. Following Mr. Sloth will bring you to poverty. Don't worry about getting wet; you've worked in the rain before. Get out and work!" He made me feel guilty, but I still didn't want to work.

Leaving my book by the warm chair, I stepped out onto the porch. Through a break in the clouds, the sun seemed to shout something to Mr. Industry, who challenged me, "At least, spread *one* wheelbarrow of chips before dinner."

Mr. Sloth didn't like the idea, but considered the prospect. He wasn't opposed to occasional tasks that boosted his opinion of himself. "I did one wheelbarrow," he could say with pride to anyone who might accuse him of laziness.

I listened to Industry. Grabbing the pitchfork, I threw it into the barrow and headed for the pile. Mr. Sloth didn't like my springy step. He complained, "Hey, not so fast! Watch out for your back! You are too old. Why don't you hire the neighbor kid?"

Mr. Industry responded, "A little exercise will loosen those back muscles. You are starting to feel good. Look! The wheelbarrow is already full!"

The first load didn't cover much area. Mr. Sloth used that fact to urge me back to my study. "This job is too big," he complained. "Besides, our agreement was *one* load."

Standing still, I slowly filled my lungs with as much fresh air as they could hold. Mr. Industry insisted, "We just have to get *another* load!" I grabbed the handles and headed for the pile. Mr. Sloth, who had been lying on the ground beside the wheelbarrow, reached up. Grabbing the edge with one hand, he hung on as I dragged him along.

I filled, pushed, dumped, and spread. My whole body had accepted Mr. Industry's advice and enjoyed it! Occasionally some limb or muscle complained of overexertion. But I kept going, load after load, in spite of Sloth's low whines.

When the final wheelbarrow load covered the last corner, I could hardly believe it. I never thought I could do the whole job so quickly! Mr. Industry let out a victorious cheer. He jumped and hollered as if I had just won the Boston Marathon! I looked around for Mr. Sloth. For the first time all day, I couldn't see him anywhere.

From the dining room window, my wife announced, "Dinner!" I put away the tools and with a light step entered the house.

All evening, Mr. Industry hung pictures of the garden victory in my mind. We rejoiced as much as any winner can. A task accomplished is sweet to the soul.

Howard applied names to his conflicting thoughts and desires. You have similar thoughts and desires whether you name them or not, and you will have them the rest of your life. The desires you follow determine the man you will become.

The path of Mr. Sloth is a flat trail, a wide trail, and I must add, a very pleasant-looking trail. He claims that it is the best of roads to travel, and the easiest. He lures you with comforts. He entices you with "little" soft choices. He would never say, "Let's sleep all day." But he might suggest, "Sleep for only ten more minutes." If you yield to that, he will encourage you to sleep for another ten minutes. By making little decisions one after another, you might find

yourself doing something that you never would have agreed to if you were presented the opportunity all at once, like sleeping the whole day. Every opportunity to make a soft choice has another opportunity right behind it.

If you accept Mr. Sloth's advice and begin this path, it will be smooth, just as he said. It might even have flowers along the borders and a bubbling brook. Walking along, you begin to see blackberry bushes sprouting in the bark mulch on both sides, just little sprouts. They gradually grow larger. As you continue, the path becomes choked with briars until you can go no farther. Turning around to go back, you are shocked! The brambles grew across the trail behind you. Following Mr. Sloth led you into the middle of a thorny blackberry patch higher than your head.

A man named Kevin knows what it is like to be in the middle of a briar patch. On a walk with his family they came upon a plum tree. Reaching for a high plum, Kevin failed to see the slope behind him. He stepped back over the edge and, with everyone watching, executed a double back flip into the briars. *Yeeeeooooouch!* If Kevin lay still, it didn't hurt much. But the slightest movement brought stabbing pain. Regardless of the pain, he had to get out; he couldn't lie still forever. Kevin grabbed the end of the dog leash that his family threw to him. Pulling and scrambling, he got out of his trap. Sure, it hurt. Yes, he did bleed, but he got out.

Just like Kevin's escape, there is only one way out of Mr. Sloth's thorny bed. You must go through it. Getting out of a slothful mentality requires choosing what is right to do, what is good to do, with a proper disregard for pain. Men without courage, and those committed to laziness, never get out. They spend the rest of their lives being pricked with ever-growing thorns.

The path of Mr. Industry begins like a blackberry patch. You grab a machete and begin to hack an aisle. Your muscles tire, you breathe hard. Suddenly you find yourself on a paved road, surrounded by a cheering crowd. Mr. Industry, Mr. Courage, Miss Cheerful, and a host of others join your progress. What once looked impossible turns into reality, when you attack it with a mind to work. The happiness that Howard and Mr. Industry enjoyed is never found by lying around on the couch. Genuine happiness dwells with a job well done.

Every day you have the desire to be industrious. Every day you have the desire to be slothful. Some days one desire is stronger than the other. The desires you follow determine the man you will become.

The way of the slothful man is as a hedge of thorns: but the way of the righteous is made plain (Proverbs 15:19).

Questions

- Howard experienced two different thoughts. What were they?

- Which one appears easier to follow?

- Can you think of a specific time when you followed Mr. Industry? Mr. Sloth?

- Imagine your mother or father just drove into the driveway. How would you feel if you had been lying around and hadn't done the job they had asked you to do? How would you feel if you had washed the dishes and cleaned your room without being asked?

- At the end of life, who will be more joyful: the slothful or the industrious?

Only a life lived for others is a life worthwhile.

—Albert Einstein

Inventions

Questions, questions, questions. Thomas continually asked questions. What makes a hot air balloon fly? How does a chicken hatch an egg? How does hydrogen combine with oxygen to make water? When no one could answer his questions, he experimented to find the answers.

Mrs. Edison, Thomas's mother, enrolled him in the local school when he was seven years old. His teacher did not like boys to ask questions and punished those who did. When Mrs. Edison learned that the teacher had labeled her son as an empty brain, she ended his school career and taught him herself.

World Book Encyclopedia says, "Mrs. Edison had the notion, unusual for those times, that learning could be fun. She made a game of teaching him—she called it exploring the exciting world of knowledge—soon he began to learn so fast that his mother could no longer teach him." From then on, he was on his own.

Thomas didn't study separate subjects throughout the day. He combined all subjects, attempting to answer the questions in his mind. As his knowledge grew and his questions were answered, he began to apply his understanding to the needs and situations in his life. Thomas Edison had become an inventor.

All boys are created with the desire to invent. Whenever they need what they don't have, their minds click into the inventor mode. They look at the problem, scrounge around for any materials they might find, then put together their ideas and materials to try to solve the problem. It is said that necessity is the mother of invention. That means that whenever a boy needs something, he tries to think up some way to get it or build it, and occasionally he invents an entirely new solution.

A good inventor needs the ability to think in analogies. He needs eyes to see the similarities between two

completely different subjects. The Bible tells slothful men to learn to work by watching ants. Ants and men are two different things, but they have a similarity. The similarity is the analogy. Ants, without being told, work when it's harvest time. When there is something to gather, they go get it. A diligent man, without being told, works just like the ants.

The slothful man doesn't consider times and seasons. Instead of picking his raspberries when they are ripe, he might wait a few weeks. When he does go out, he works harder for fewer berries because most have rotted. If the slothful man wants to learn what he did wrong, God tells him to go watch the ants and apply what he sees to his own life. That is learning to think in analogies. God filled the world with analogies, and He desires men to seek for them. As Proverbs says, "It is the glory of God to conceal a thing: but the honor of kings is to search out a matter."

George de Mestral was a boy who liked to search out matters. He grew up in Switzerland in the early 1900s. He loved the outdoors and loved inventing. At twelve years of age, he received his first patent for inventing a toy airplane. His early successes made him want to study engineering to help him design more new things.

God is the best engineer of all and displays His skill in nature. George watched carefully and learned from what he saw. After a day of hunting, he spent hours pulling pesky burrs from his wool pants and his dog's fur. Wondering why they stuck, he put one under his microscope. He found each burr to be made of hundreds of tiny hooks that locked onto the loops of fabric and fur when pressed together. George decided to take this lesson from nature and apply its wisdom to an everyday useful product. In 1951 he applied for a patent. Today we have hook and loop tape, commonly known as Velcro. All over the world, people enjoy quick and secure latches for shoes, coats, tools, and hundreds of other products because George de Mestral saw the relationship between an annoying weed and a practical need in life.

The ability to think in analogies can turn useless objects into useful tools. In my shop are two drawers I call my invention drawers. They are stuffed with old drills, metal scraps, leather straps, springs, and even some Velcro. Everything in there is just one step away from the garbage can, useless by itself. When I need to make a new jig or special tool, I dig around in those drawers. Often items that were once used for one reason may be combined to form something completely new. Taking a worthless scrap and applying it in a new way to my current need has given me some great tools.

If you want to increase your ability to invent, practice combining knowledge from different subjects. When you study about Hannibal, the great general from Carthage, don't leave him in the dusty archives of an old book. Add his genius to your life. Ask yourself, how can I use his military tactics when I fight my battles, whether on the football field, the chess board, or in my heart and mind?

Godly men founded the United States government. When you study the history and current function of that government, think in analogies. Bring the ideas to life. For example: The Department of Transportation oversees the roads, trains, ships, and airplanes in our country. Their goal is safe and efficient travel. Imagine yourself as the Secretary of Transportation in your home. What do you have for transportation? It might be your skateboard, a bicycle, or the car. Are you fulfilling your responsibility to oversee their maintenance? Do you keep the stairs and hallways clear, providing safe travel for your family as they walk the "roads" of the house?

Early in Edison's career, he invented a machine for Congress that would speed up the voting process. When he presented it, they said they didn't need it. They liked stretching out the voting time and didn't want any new machines to hurry them along! Right there he purposed to never again invent anything that nobody wanted. Edison devoted himself to what he called "the desperate needs of the world."

How do you know what those "desperate needs" are? The Bible is the best textbook for setting an inventor on the right track. The needs of men and the beginning, the end, and the purpose of life are clearly described.

Start with that Book. Then explore nature. Add to that all the knowledge, investigation, and experimentation available. As you face needs that arise before you, and prayerfully think about them, you will find answers, invent products, and develop solutions to meet those needs.

God, the Great Inventor, gives men boundaries for inventions. Never invent anything evil, not even an evil thought! All new creations of men must find a place under these two great rules: Love God with all your heart, and love your neighbor as yourself.

What should your attitude be when your invention fails? While attempting to develop a storage battery, Edison attempted ten thousand experiments that failed. He was not discouraged. He now had ten thousand ways not to go. Don't give up if you fail. Learn from the mistake and try again. Keep going; you will find the answer.

God created you with the desire to invent. Songs, programs, products, methods, art, literature, and tools are waiting to be invented by you. An abundance of information fills our world today, but few men stop to consider how to turn that information into useful products and ideas that free men to serve God with all their hearts. Think in analogies. Become the inventor God created you to be. Meet the desperate needs of the world.

> *I wisdom dwell with prudence, and find out knowledge of witty inventions* (Proverbs 8:12).

Questions

- Why did Thomas Edison not fit in at school?

- What one skill is very useful for inventing?

- What gave George de Mestral the idea to invent hook and loop tape?

- What is the Christian's goal for his inventions? Why invent?

[Justice] is placed before mercy...
in the Scriptures, and just men are in
many parts of the inspired writings
placed upon very high ground. It is
right it should be so. The world
stands in more need of justice than
charity, and indeed it is the want of
justice that renders charity every-
where so necessary.

—Benjamin Rush to John Adams, 1811

Justice

Justice is the backbone of a man. It gives him the ability to face all his selfish passions, to knock them to the side of the road, and to walk forward, doing what is right.

At the hobby store Robby found the rocket of his dreams. But when he looked at the price, he found that he lacked $4.95. Leaving the store, Robby saw a lady drop a piece of paper on the sidewalk. When he reached the spot, he found a five-dollar bill. *This is my lucky day! Now I can buy that rocket!* His next thought overcame his selfish passion. *This isn't my money! It belongs to that lady.* He ran to the corner in time to see the lady climbing into her car. Hurrying to her window, he knocked softly. "You dropped this," he said, holding up the bill. "Oh, thank you," was her reply. Though Robby didn't get his rocket, he received more joy from returning the bill than he ever would from watching a rocket launch. "It is joy to the just to do judgment" (Proverbs 21:15).

Travis and Ben were playing in the parking lot behind the grocery store. They came there almost every day to throw a tennis ball against the block wall and practice catching grounders. Today a magazine on the pavement was flapping in the wind. Travis went over to pick it up. He could tell that it was one of those magazines that perverted men like to read. He wanted to turn the pages and see what was in it, but his dad had taught him justice. Before he gave in to his selfish desires, he walked straight to the dumpster, threw the magazine where it belonged, and continued fielding grounders. The delight in his heart over doing what was right far exceeded any pleasure that he might find in looking at obscene pictures. "It is joy to the just to do judgment."

Justice is a protective wall that guards a boy from selfishness and directs him to what is right. Without it, a boy becomes a slave to his appetites, a puppet to his lusts. He might get what he wants now, but he will grow to regret it later. With justice, a boy is shielded from all that destroys and is kept for all that is useful and good.

Justice is simply giving what is due, to whom it is due, when it is due. Robby gave the five dollars to the lady who dropped it, as soon as he could. That's justice. Travis gave the trashy magazine to the dumpster where it belonged, as quickly as possible. That's justice.

It is easy to distinguish between just and unjust boys. The just think about what they owe to others. The unjust think about what others owe to them. The just consider how to pay what they owe, while the unjust avoid paying.

What does a just boy owe? Often it is something besides money. When he is playing on a baseball team, he owes them his total effort. When he works for the neighbor, he owes a full hour's work for a full hour's pay. He owes honor and obedience to his parents. To his teachers he owes respect and all the studying they require. To his city he owes compliance to laws. He owes love to every person he meets. To God, a just boy owes his whole life.

Unjust boys believe that everyone owes them something. They are often upset, thinking about what they didn't get. The coach didn't play them as much as he should have. Their friend didn't give them a birthday present. They should have won the door prize. Their life is a constant complaint.

The unjust take what God gives and spend it on themselves. They give the time God gave for studying to playing Frisbee. They give their energy to shooting baskets instead of completing their chores. They give their savings to the dollar store for a cheap toy instead of putting it in their bank account. When they should use their talents to glorify God, they waste them on selfish pleasures. Even when the unjust make an attempt to pay their debts, they are often unable for they have misspent the provisions God has given them and are broke.

The just know who they owe. They also know who they don't owe. The just owe nothing to their selfish lusts and pride. When they face a desire to steal, they don't have to give it a second thought. The answer is no! When they feel the desire to brag about how fast they ran the hundred-yard dash, they don't even give it a place on their tongue. Instead they compliment the other runners.

By experience, the just learn one of life's great secrets: It is a joy to pay what you owe. If you are sitting around feeling bored and want something to perk you up, think about some debt you owe and go pay it. As you were leaving Mrs. Nelson's house, she asked you to come again. You said that you would, but you haven't been back for weeks. Pay up! Brighten her day with a visit. Maybe you owe your music lessons an hour today. Pay up! Get in there. Practice like a man. Give it your whole heart. The actual act of paying a debt isn't always fun, but the satisfaction of paying it far outweighs the work. "It is joy to the just to do judgment."

God delights in the just. He is always looking for a just man to shower special benefits upon. The man who considers the everyday people and situations in his life and pays them what he owes is the man God blesses.

Jesus is called the Just One because, throughout His life, He always paid what He owed, to whom He owed it, when He owed it. Before Jesus came, men could not enter heaven because they were unjust, according to God's laws. They didn't pay what they owed to God—they couldn't. Jesus died to pay that debt, the Just for the unjust, to bring them to God.

"It is joy to the just to do judgment." Therefore, for the joy that was set before Him, He endured the cross. Jesus received the greatest joy in the world because he paid the greatest of all debts.

"Wherefore God [who is always on the lookout for just men] also hath highly exalted him, and given him a name which is above every name: That at the name of Jesus every knee should bow...and that every tongue should confess that Jesus Christ is Lord, to the glory of God the Father" (Philippians 2:9-11). Jesus was well rewarded for His just actions.

God still looks for just men today. He gives them all the resources they need to pay what they owe, to whom they owe it, when they owe it. Will you be a man who, for the joy that is set before you, pays all of your debts?

Render therefore to all their dues: tribute to whom tribute is due; custom to whom custom; fear to whom fear; honor to whom honor. Owe no man anything, but to love one another: for he that loveth another hath fulfilled the law (Romans 13:7,8).

Questions

- What is justice?

- Why was Robby just?

- Why was Travis just?

- Jesus was called the Just One. Why?

- What is one of life's secrets mentioned in this chapter?

He didn't care if he went without a shirt on his own back, so long as the men he was leading had sufficient clothing.

—Lionel Greenstreet about Ernest Shackleton

Leadership

In 1916, Ernest Shackleton and his men approached the coast of Antarctica. They were attempting to be the first party to hike across the continent. It was a particularly cold year with more ocean ice than usual. With only one day's sail to their destination, the ocean froze around their ship, the *Endurance*.

For nearly a year, the ice held them captive before it crushed and sank the boat. The crew camped on the ice floe until it broke to pieces with the warming weather. Climbing into three small lifeboats, the twenty-eight men took to the open sea. Their desperate struggle only allowed them to reach a barren land called Elephant Island. Unless someone went for help, every man would surely die. The nearest source of help was eight hundred miles away on South George Island.

Shackelton and five of his men accepted the challenge. In a twenty-two-foot makeshift sailboat, they faced some of the most treacherous waters in the world. They battled hurricane winds and 150-foot waves. Freezing rain built up eighteen inches of ice on their small craft. Without modern navigation equipment, and with only a few good readings of their sextant, they miraculously reached the shore of South George.

From sea level, the small party had to climb a range of uncharted, snowcapped peaks to the whaling station on the other side. Exhaustion and hunger tracked them like wolves, forcing them to gamble for their lives. On a slope of sheer ice they had to make a choice: Either die from exposure or lock themselves into a human toboggan and slide down a steep slope into the fog.

Without knowing what lay at the bottom, they took the chance. Sitting in a row and screaming at the top of their lungs, they slid down the mountainside. Expecting to go over a cliff or dash themselves upon some rock wall, they were elated to find themselves stopping unharmed on a flat glacier.

Though Shackleton and his small band were saved from death by reaching the South George whaling station, he couldn't rest until all of his men were safe. It took months and four different ships, but he safely rescued every man.

Frank Worsley, captain of the *Endurance,* wrote in his book *Shackleton's Boat Journey,* "It was certain that a man of such heroic mind and self-sacrificing nature as Shackleton would undertake this most dangerous and difficult task himself. He was, in fact, unable by nature to do otherwise. He had to lead in the position of most danger, difficulty and responsibility. I have seen him turn pale, yet force himself into the post of the greatest peril. That was his type of courage; he would do the job that he was most afraid of.

"By self-sacrifice and throwing his own life into the balance he saved every one of his men—not a life was lost—although at times it had looked unlikely that one could be saved. His outstanding characteristics were his care of, and anxiety for, the lives and well-being of all his men."

Ernest Shackleton was a great leader because he looked past his own fears, his own pain, and his own distress to see the needs of his men. We need more men like Shackleton—men who look past themselves to the needs of others.

Many boys are said to be shy. Their parents explain why their son did not say thank you or hello with the excuse, "Joey is just being shy today." The truth is that Joey is just caught up in himself. Joey thinks too much of his own feelings and thoughts to consider someone else. Joey is simply selfish.

When a selfish boy arrives at a birthday party, his thoughts naturally revolve around himself. He is not sure if he wants to be there. *I bet they don't like me. What's to eat? What are we doing for fun?*

A boy destined to be a leader will ask himself different questions: *Is anyone sad? How can I cheer them? Is anyone lonely? Could I help by sitting near them?* He sees someone needing a chair and gets one. He asks the hostess, "What can I do to help?" He begins conversations with those that look uncomfortable. He thinks so much of others that he may overlook getting cake and punch for himself.

The selfish boy leaves the party with the same thoughts he brought. *So-and-so didn't like me. No one took an interest in me. The cake wasn't sweet enough. I didn't win any prizes.*

The future leader leaves with his thoughts full of the people he met and the opportunities he had to serve. He didn't really notice the cake; it was good enough. He didn't care about winning any prizes and was delighted to see Harry get that pocketknife. Harry had told him how he had lost one just a week ago!

The budding leader might have developed a new area of interest. The man he brought a chair to told him all about his desert travels. He described the thrill of a sunrise, the extreme quietness followed by the choir of birds and then the indescribable colors! The boy had never known such a glorious thing existed! He was going to check the atlas to find the nearest desert.

A selfish boy doesn't have to remain one all his life. He can grow out of it. He can mature to be someone like

Shackleton who will risk his life for the sake of his men. Where does a boy start?

Start by asking God for eyes to see the needs of people. A simple prayer might be: "Dear God, I am selfish. I think more about me than anyone. I know this is not what You want for me. Will you open my eyes to see the needs of others, so that I can help them? This is the way that You are, and I want to be like You. Amen."

Next, really look at people around you each day. Take moments and think, *What does Dad feel like when he comes home? How can I help him? What makes him glad?* Or, *What does Mom feel like when she gets up in the morning? What can I do to make her day brighter?*

When you meet people, be attentive. Are they happy or sad, tired or energetic? Why do they feel that way? Make it a game to understand their hearts. Then, laugh with those who laugh and cry with those who cry.

When you enter a room or visit someone's house, be on the lookout for helpful things to do. You can sit in the corner

and selfishly hope that someone will notice you, or you can embark on an adventure looking for people to serve. Developing an eye for service brings freedom from fear and selfishness. You forget your shyness, your hurts, and your own sadness as you help others. Every true leader has the vision for serving.

Do you want to be a man with courage like Shackelton? Your biggest hindrance is selfishness. The selfish are not courageous. You must become a man who thinks of others. It is not waiting for some big chance to save lives that makes a hero; a hero is made by thinking of others in everyday situations.

The choice is before you. Will you be a selfish coward or will you be like Ernest Shackleton, a courageous leader whose eyes saw the needs of his men?

Look not every man on his own things, but
every man also on the things of others
(Philippians 2:4).

Questions

- Can you find Elephant and South George Islands on a globe or atlas?

- What is another word for *shy*?

- What was Ernest Shackleton's secret for being a great leader?

- What can you do to develop leadership skills?

The world is so full of a number of things;
I'm sure we should all be as happy as kings.

—Robert Louis Stevenson

Learn to Like It!

While shopping for tennis shoes in the mall, Frank listened to the radio blaring from the intercom system.

"Ladies and gentlemen, welcome to the *What's New in Kalamazoo* program, here on KGRQ radio. I'm your host, Johnny Wells. Tonight we have with us none other than Fat Freddie himself! Freddie is the owner of Kalamazoo's newest eating establishment, Fat Freddie's Food Factory! Freddie, tell us about your new restaurant."

Freddie took the microphone and began: "Thanks, Johnny, for inviting me to the station today. It's great to be here. As you know, I've been building my restaurant for two years, and tonight..." here Freddie took a deep breath, "tonight is the grand opening of Fat Freddie's Food Factory on the corner of Fourth and Franklin! And, for only four dollars and forty-five cents, the first four hundred forty-five famished faces filling the forty-five-foot foyer may freely follow fat fastidious Freddie through four hundred forty-five feet of fabulous foods, fashioned by Freddie's favorite fifty-four frolicking food handlers, for the foremost finicky foragers!"

When Freddie finished, he fell flat on a folded futon, gasping for air. (If you think Freddie's a weakling, try reading that announcement in one breath yourself! Be sure you are standing near a futon when you attempt it!)

Johnny, a veteran announcer, didn't miss a beat. Grabbing the microphone as Freddie collapsed, and acting as if nothing had happened, he said, "Well, folks, there you have it from Freddie himself. Get yourself down to Fourth and Franklin by five tonight and be one of those first four hundred forty-five folks to feast at Fat Freddie's Food Factory. Tune in again next week for another installment of *What's New in Kalamazoo!*"

Frank could hardly believe his ears. Freddie's was just down the street from his home. All summer he'd waited for the grand opening, and tonight was the night! "I've got to go!" he said aloud.

Forgetting about the tennis shoes, Frank dashed home. The screen door slammed behind him as he bolted into the kitchen. "Hey, Dad! Fat Freddie's Food Factory is open tonight! May we go?"

"Sure, Frank!" said Dad, when he heard the news. "Let's do it!"

Dad liked supporting local businesses. He also liked being in the front row of any excitement. It was no surprise to his family when he announced, "Let's get there at four and be the first in line!"

At five o'clock sharp, Fat Freddie opened the door, handed Frank an enormous plate and, throwing both of his arms high in the air, proclaimed, "Let the festivities begin!"

You have never seen anything like it! Four counters, each four hundred forty-five feet long, were filled with Freddie's finest foods.

Mother and Father overloaded their plates within forty yards of the front door. They began looking for a seat. Frank found nothing that he liked yet. With an empty plate in hand, he continued down the aisle.

Freddie had painted the floor with a stripe every ten yards, making it look like a football field. Frank was on the forty, then the fifty. Freddie followed him to the sixty-, seventy-, and eighty-yard lines. Still, Frank found nothing he liked!

Freddie couldn't believe his ears as he heard Frank say, "I don't like that. Those don't look good. Yuck!" Frank walked the entire Food Factory without finding one item that he liked to eat!

Fat Freddie was beside himself. "What do you mean; you don't like any of it? What else could there be?"

"Creamy peanut butter with strawberry jelly on white balloon bread," whined Frank.

"You have got to be kidding!" screamed Freddie. "Almost everything in the world is in front of you. And you are whining for the one thing I don't serve!"

"Do you have any cheese-flavored cocoa corn flakes?" asked Frank.

Fat Freddie was never good at controlling his emotions. He staggered and fell backward into the lemonade fountain.

When Dad and Mom heard the commotion and saw Frank with an empty plate at the end of the line, they knew what had happened. Frank *was* a picky eater. Throwing down their knives and forks, they sprinted the hundred yards to Frank and dragged him out the back door just before a reporter could capture the event for the local newspaper. How embarrassing that would have been.

Frank walked home with his parents, discontented, complaining, and hungry.

Four of Freddie's favorite food handlers fished him out of the lemonade fountain. Sloshing toward the back room, Freddie desperately tried to understand how a boy could walk past four hundred forty-five feet of meats, salads, drinks, dinner rolls, casseroles, vegetables, pastas, fruits, seafood, puddings, soft drinks, ice cream, and pies without liking any of it!

Of course, Freddie and Frank are imaginary characters. Do you think that there are any Franks in real life? Do you complain about the food fixed for you? Do you like your chores? Do you like the people in your life, your lessons, your clothes, and your bedroom? Whenever we don't like our share of life, we are just like Frank!

"The world is so full of a number of things; I'm sure we should all be as happy as kings." But are we? Have you ever said, "I don't like work. I don't like rain. I don't like it when it's hot. I don't like the cold. I don't like the city. I don't like the country. I don't like… I don't like… I don't like…"?

If you desire to enjoy the bountiful life God has given, you must learn to like it. You have the choice. Either complain and murmur about life or develop a taste for it. Most people choose to murmur and complain. But you don't have to.

I didn't like onions. My wife does, and she purposely put onions in foods that she made for me. Whenever I found a bit of onion I complained, "What is this doing in my food?"

After eating my wife's cooking for many years, I've learned to like onions. I even miss them if they're left out of my burritos!

I wonder why I didn't like onions when I was young. Instead of holding my nose, I could have enjoyed hundreds of dishes that my mom and my wife prepared for me.

Of course, we should never want to like what is evil. And there are some unhealthy things that we should avoid. However, we make detours in disgust around countless good things we could enjoy, if we only changed our attitude.

Becoming a mature man means learning to like all parts of life, the hard parts and the easy parts, the sour and the sweet. A practical classroom for learning to like life is the dinner table. Here is a challenge for you: pick a healthy food that you don't care for and learn to like it. Don't just learn to tolerate it; learn to look forward to it!

I can't expect you to accept this challenge if I'm not willing to. I don't like ranch dressing. There is no good reason. I just don't. I've never even bothered to try it because I am convinced I don't like it.

While writing this chapter, I am reminded to stop living like Frank. So if you and I ever meet, please ask me, "How do you like ranch dressing?" It will be a good motivation for me. By then I'm going to like it.

We should learn to enjoy life not only for ourselves— it is also a great benefit to the people we live with. Often we hurt others by our picky attitudes.

Growing up, my family didn't have much money. One Christmas, my mother bought me a brown corduroy jacket with a sheepskin lining. She sacrificed for that coat. Watching me open the package, she could tell that I didn't like it in spite of my polite "thank you." Nobody wore jackets like that. It hung in my closet. My mom wanted to please me, but I couldn't bring myself to like an out-of-style jacket. She cried because she felt like a failure.

A few years later, after I got rid of the coat, brown corduroy jackets came into style. I liked them then. Why couldn't I have been a son who cared more about my mom's heart than about the style of my jacket?

God offers us a grand life. Are we backing down from it, or are we diving into it with pleasure? Let's not live like Frank, turning up our noses at the wonderful things God has given us just because we don't have a taste for them.

"Please pass the ranch dressing."

> *He that is of a merry heart hath a continual feast* (Proverbs 15:15).

Questions

- Why did Frank leave Freddie's Food Factory hungry?
- Who decides whether you enjoy life or dislike it?
- What was the dinner table challenge?
- Are you brave enough to accept that challenge?
- Have you tried reading Freddie's announcement with only one breath?

True worth is in being, not seeming,
In doing, each day that goes by,
Some little good, not in dreaming
Of great things to do by and by.

—Alice Cary, "Nobility"

Life Is Doing

The chickens' water trough is on the other side of the fence. I can stick a hose through the wire to fill it. To clean it out, I have to walk around the dog run, the rabbit yard, and the chicken house, duck under a low gate and cut across the chicken yard. For three years I have said to myself, "I would like a gate here." Last month I finally realized that all the wishing in the world would not build a gate for me. I had only a few minutes that day, but they were enough to look around for some hinges, wire, and a few two-by-fours. I set them at the far end of the porch, ready for a day when I had more time.

Within a week I found a spare hour. Out to the pen I went. In less than sixty minutes, I built a new gate. Now, I can easily keep the chickens' water clean. "Desire accomplished is sweet to the soul" (Proverbs 13:19).

A slothful man always wants something that he never receives. He never gets it because he never does anything about it. He wanted it last year. He wants it this year. He will want it next year. At the end of his life, he will still be wishing that he had done something about it. A diligent man considers his desires. If his desires are good, he starts today to accomplish them. It may be only a little work today, only a little tomorrow, but in time he gets what he wants—by working for it.

In our society, life has turned into a spectator sport. A spectator sport is one where most of the people watch and only a few people actually do something. Professional football is an example of a spectator sport. Millions of people watch twenty-two other people play a game. Americans like to watch movies. Millions of people will watch a few people act out a made-up life. Americans like to listen to music. Millions of people will listen to one person sing or play an instrument. Even in churches, millions

of people will watch one person minister to others. Many people go through life watching and listening to other people live, instead of getting out and living themselves.

No boy grows into useful manhood with a spectator attitude towards life. Sitting on a couch watching other people do things is a sure road to slothfulness. He begins to desire things that he will never get, because he is sitting instead of doing.

A society of spectators breeds bored people. The people doing things find fulfillment in life. Those who get off the couch to invent new products, who learn useful skills, and who fulfill their responsibilities are the people who find the abundant joyful life.

You can dream about a life of adventure or you can live one. Sitting around wishing will never accomplish your dreams.

One practical way to develop a doer's attitude is to look around and see the things that need to be done in your home. Is there anything that could be done before it is time to go to bed? Are there any light bulbs that need to be changed? Is there oil for that squeaky hinge? Is your bedroom orderly? Ask Mom, Dad, or maybe your sister, "Is there something I could do for you?"

Do you dream of being an engineer? Get out a book on math or science and begin to study tonight. Herbert Hoover learned math on his own during the evenings after work. When he took an entrance exam for engineering college, he did so well in math that they overlooked his low scores in other subjects and let him in. His everyday diligence paved his life's road all the way to the presidency of the United States. Whatever you dream about, do something today to begin the process.

We were created to be doers, not watchers. A boy of action is useful and productive. His dad rejoices because his son sees the things needing attention in the yard and does them without being asked. His mom smiles because he practices his instrument without a reminder. He lives his dreams instead of thinking them. He enjoys the privileges of the diligent and avoids the bored longings of the slothful.

Go and live. Study, work, build, invest; be about life! Don't get caught watching life go by.

But be ye doers of the word, and not hearers only, deceiving your own selves (James 1:22).

Questions

- What is a spectator sport?

- What is a slothful man always doing?

- What makes a diligent man happy?

- Is there something you want to accomplish in your lifetime?

- How can you start today?

...surely there are some who feel that life is infinitely important; who know that they are placed here to gain good and to do good; who remember that the only opportunities they have for both are short and uncertain: surely these will not sleep as do others—surely these will feel the excitement and reproach. It is high time to awake out of sleep: they that sleep, sleep in the night.

—Reverend William Jay, *Morning Exercises*

Meeting God in the Morning

Shortly after getting up this morning, I read two verses from the Bible which reminded me of a day, years ago, that I spent in the lava fields of the Three Sisters Wilderness. The Three Sisters, named Faith, Hope, and Love, are major peaks in the Cascade mountain range of the Pacific Northwest. Surrounding these mountains are cinder cones, craters, and wide rivers of jagged black lava. The whole wilderness area is a witness to the violent volcanic eruptions that took place a few thousand years ago.

That particular day I sat for hours beside an old snag of a tree in the middle of those lava fields. All was deathly still, except for the wind and an occasional caw of a distant raven.

On the first Monday of each month, I usually go some place where God and I enjoy the day together. We often pick a remote spot, one where God really shows off His handiwork. I read my Bible slowly, pausing occasionally to look at the magnificent scenery. He inspires me with His Words and works. I pray to Him, He speaks to my heart. When stiff from sitting, I walk. When tired, I sleep. By the end of the day I am refreshed, reminded of my responsibilities, and assured that He is in control of everything in the world.

The verses I read that day were Psalm 71:17,18: "O God, thou hast taught me from my youth: and hitherto have I declared thy wondrous works. Now also when I am old and grayheaded, O God, forsake me not; until I have shown thy strength unto this generation, and thy power to every one that is to come."

I thought about the future and wondered if I would live to have gray hair. And if I did, what things would I want to tell the next generation about God's strength?

Many years have gone by. My hair is now gray. God has done many things to show His strength to me. One stands out above them all: Throughout my life, God has shown His strength to me by faithfully drawing me out of bed each morning that *He* might enjoy a relationship with me.

Some people see early rising as a difficult discipline reserved for the hardy, self-controlled person. For me, it isn't a discipline; it is a gift from a living God to a weak man.

I was taught that a Christian young man was supposed to get up early in the morning and have devotions. It was my duty. It may have been my duty, but it was also my struggle. One morning, when I was about eighteen years old, I had a particularly difficult fight and was losing. I tried and tried to get up, but I couldn't do it.

Then I heard God's voice in my heart saying, "Quit trying—and get up."

It startled me. Not that I would hear God's voice in my heart, but that the idea was so simple. I quit trying and got up!

Though I quit fighting and faithfully got up in the mornings, I often experienced dullness. My mind wandered. My eyes lost focus. I fell back asleep trying to do my duty to God—reading His Bible and recording truths in my journal. I didn't give up. I continued the struggle because that is what a man is supposed to do.

God, who thoroughly understands us, knows that each of us can easily get up when there is something exciting waiting for us. I remember being asked when I was thirteen years old, "Would you like to ride with me in the log truck tomorrow?"

"I sure would!"

"Be ready to go at three."

"I will," I answered, and I was. At thirteen, the chance to spend a day on a logging landing, in the mill yard and on the road in between was too great to pass up for a few hours of sleep.

"Do you want to go skiing tomorrow?" they asked.

"I sure would!"

"We'll pick you up at four-thirty."

"I'll be ready." And I was. At twenty, the opportunity to spend the day on the slopes of Mt. Bachelor was too great to pass up for a few hours of sleep. A reason to get up, like skiing, made it easy.

God knew that I was willing to get up in the mornings. His next step was to give me a reason to get up, far more exciting than any log truck ride or ski trip. I remember the night when I was not looking forward to dull devotions in the morning. I spoke to God as I climbed into bed. "I'm tired. I don't want to get up in the morning for the sake of duty. If You want to spend time with me, wake me at four and make me alert."

The next morning, I felt something inside of me, a short, faint "bing." I sensed being awake. I opened my eyes, looking straight at the clock. To the second, it was exactly FOUR A.M. My God wanted me!

From that day forward, there was no thought of duty or devotions. My God, the One who created everything in the world, wanted to meet with me. He wanted to hear my concerns, my dreams, and my fears. He wanted to share His concerns, His dreams, and His heart with me. He gave me words to encourage people, warnings to curb my wayward actions, and wisdom for daily life.

If you knew that the president of the United States wanted to come to your house tomorrow to talk with you about the affairs of the nation, would you get up to meet him? Of course you would! Would it take discipline to get you up? No! With the excitement and the honor of having the president in your home, the question isn't whether you could get up in the morning. The question is whether you could sleep at all during the night! There is One far greater than the president who wants to meet with you and discuss the affairs of His Kingdom each morning.

I cannot imagine life without the morning hours God and I spend together. He likes it more than I do. We don't have devotions, we have a relationship. The anticipation of experiencing Him draws me out of bed. How can a man lie in bed when the Creator wants to talk with him? It is not to the man's credit that he gets up; the credit goes to the One who calls the man.

There are a few things I've learned about getting up early in the morning. One is that God created sleep. His normal design is that people sleep each night. Some mornings my first thought is, "He giveth His beloved sleep" (Psalm 127:2). When these words follow an unusually interrupted or sleepless night, I receive them as God's encouragement to me. I confidently roll over and continue sleeping.

All people need sleep, but not every one needs the same amount. Don't let anyone belittle you if you need more than they do. And don't expect others to be like you if you get along with less. True spirituality is not measured by who gets up first in the morning. If God wakes you, what do you have to brag about?

Another issue: What do you do when you know you should have gotten up, but you overslept? You didn't mean to sleep that long! Now it is too late to quietly meet with God because you must fulfill your daily obligations. When this happens, do you scold yourself for several hours? Do you feel your whole day is ruined? Do you imagine that God refuses to walk with you that day? I have done all of those. And none of them is helpful. I've learned that when I fail, the best recovery is to get out of bed, promptly admit my fault, commit myself to Him, and walk in His presence. The goal isn't the meeting; the goal is the relationship. Maybe I missed the meeting; but I am not going to miss the relationship.

As a gray-headed man who has spent more than ten thousand mornings with my God, I want to declare to the next generation: The greatest event in my life is meeting with God in the mornings. He is strong enough to draw a weak man out of bed. God is also personal enough not only to listen to my heart, but to share His with me.

God, the Creator of your being, wants to draw you to Himself. Will you let Him?

The Lord hath appeared of old unto me, saying, Yea, I have loved thee with an everlasting love: therefore with loving kindness have I drawn thee (Jeremiah 31:3).

Questions

- What should you do when you are "trying" to get up in the morning, but can't?

- Who wants a relationship most—you with God or God with you?

- Why does God want to meet with you?

- What should you do if you intended to get up but failed?

If you can keep your head when all about you
Are losing theirs and blaming it on you;
...you'll be a Man, my son!

—Rudyard Kipling, "If"

Misunderstood

He parked the motorcycle and waited. I saw him as I drove by. Why do I always jump a little inside when I see a policeman? A quick look at my speedometer assured me that I wasn't speeding.

"Yikes!" I thought, "here he comes." I turned onto the freeway, so did he! What did I do wrong? The policeman came alongside my truck. He yelled at me. I couldn't hear him. I yelled back. Unable to hear me, he turned on his blue flashing lights and motioned me to the shoulder.

We spoke excitedly to one another for a few minutes. Friends drove past on their way to work.

"You know what this looks like?" I asked.

"No, it doesn't," he returned.

"Yes, it does," I argued.

"No, it doesn't," he insisted. "When a policeman is giving a ticket, he doesn't park his motorcycle beside the truck. He parks behind it."

"You might know that, Doug," I said, "But I've never known that. And I imagine that my friends driving by and snickering don't know that either."

It really didn't matter. Doug Jordan and I were two old friends having a good time. We hadn't seen each other in years. Twenty minutes passed while the lights flashed, the motorcycle sat by my door, and more friends drove by.

The following day my family and I drove to the small town of Oakridge. In my rearview mirror, I saw a car approaching quickly. Following him was a police car with its lights flashing. "Hey, that guy behind us is just about to get a ticket!" I announced. Then I remembered Doug, "Well, maybe it's just two old friends about to have a good chat!"

What do you think when you see a policeman pulling over a car? I usually think that the driver has broken the law and is going to get a warning or a ticket. If someone thought Doug was ticketing me, they were wrong. They misunderstood because they didn't know proper police procedure either.

Throughout life you will be misunderstood. Some misunderstandings are funny, some are small. Some destroy families, and some can even cost you your life. Know this: you will be misunderstood.

My wife and I were staying in a tent-like structure called a yurt at the Umpqua Lighthouse State Park on the Oregon coast. While sitting at the table eating dinner, we could hear the family from the next yurt returning from a walk. Their twelve-year-old boy ran ahead. Up onto our porch he came at full speed. His happy face turned to disgust as he looked into our window. "What are you doing in my yurt?" His glaring eyes exclaimed. With a fork of potato salad up to my lips, my eyes said to him, "What are you doing looking in my window?" You should have been there to see his face change from indignation to inquiry, to embarrassment, to fear; then his face disappeared altogether. We laughed as we heard him return to his mother and gasp, "I went to the wrong one!"

How do you respond when someone misunderstands you? Are you offended? Do you get mad? Do you stomp off to your room and refuse to talk? Or do you quietly speak the truth and keep doing all the good you can? If you respond wisely when someone misunderstands you, it is because you are able to see a bigger picture. You see past your pride to the value of a relationship, or you see the worth of a more important goal.

I remember one time when being understood didn't matter at all because there was something more important that I wanted. I arrived at the Oregon Department of Motor Vehicles promptly after my sixteenth birthday, eager for my driving test. Besides hours of practice, I knew everything in the driving manual. I also had a magazine article entitled "Driving Tips" by Parnelli Jones, the famous race car driver. With Parnelli, I had all the advice I'd ever need to be an expert driver. Here is a prime example: When the driver in front of you turns on his left blinker, move slightly to the right to allow the driver behind you to see the turn signal in front of you. During the driving test my opportunity to show off arrived. The left tail light of the yellow Ford in front of me began blinking. Confidently, I steered slightly to the right. Out of the corner of my eye I tried to see the tester's reaction to my superb driving. Certainly he knew about Parnelli Jones. "I might even get extra credit," I thought.

A score of 70 out of a possible 100 was required to pass the test. I wondered how many people ever got 110 points. After driving the course, the tester sat me down for the results. "I am giving you a score of 70," he began. "I deducted 10 points when you lost control of your car as you stopped behind the yellow Ford."

What? I couldn't believe my ears! I felt indignant. I should be getting extra points instead of losing ten! In spite of my poor attitude, I had enough sense to see the bigger picture. This man had the power to give or withhold my driver's license. I was only one point away from failing! It didn't matter if that tester understood Parnelli or not. My desire to get a license overcame my desire to blurt out, "You don't understand!"

One main purpose of our life is to display the glory of God. Reflecting God's glory is more important than being understood. Responding to misunderstanding with anger, and cutting off relationships, displays the nature of evil rather than the nature of Him who created us. The desire to see God glorified allows us to overlook misunderstandings and false accusations. It motivates us to hold our tongues, to speak the truth, and to do all the good we can. Misunderstandings are opportunities to show God's attitudes, such as patience, forgiveness, and humility.

Jesus Christ is the example of a mature man. He knows how to act when falsely accused. He is misunderstood more than anyone in history. Simon Peter, the fisherman, spent three years with Jesus. He saw Him respond to angry accusations. Peter wrote a letter to Christians who were being falsely accused. He told them that Jesus was the model of suffering. When He was reviled, He didn't revile back. When He was threatened, He didn't return the threat. He committed himself to God who judges righteously. Peter challenged Christian men to follow Jesus' example (1 Peter 2:20-23).

When you are misunderstood or falsely accused, instead of getting mad, relax and consider what is happening. It shouldn't be a surprise that you are misunderstood. It is a common occurrence. Be confident that God understands. If He doesn't make things right today, there is a day coming when He will clear up all misunderstandings and show every motive for what it is.

Peter learned that it was God's will for Jesus to be falsely accused and to suffer unjustly. When bystanders saw the mistreatment that Jesus received and His response, they were drawn to Him. The same thing happens today. When a man suffers wrongfully and takes it patiently, he attracts the attention of those watching. Some seriously consider, "Why would he quietly suffer when he doesn't have it coming?" As they seek the answer, they are drawn to the sufferer, who can then lead them to God. Every Christian boy who patiently suffers wrong receives the privilege of displaying the character of Jesus.

Moments before Jesus' death, He continued to illustrate how to respond to false accusations. He prayed, "Father, forgive them; for they know not what they do" (Luke 23:34). Later, a man named Stephen followed His example. When falsely accused and in the act of being stoned, Stephen cried, "Lord, lay not this sin to their charge" (Acts 8:60).

The apostle Paul watched Stephen die and heard his words. When Paul was falsely accused before legal authorities, and when all his friends deserted him, Paul responded, "I pray God that it may not be laid to their charge" (2 Timothy 4:16).

After seeing these examples of Jesus, Stephen, and Paul forgiving those who misunderstood them, it is your turn. And as you forgive those who misunderstand you, others will take courage to do the same.

God's mysterious weapon, which fights against misunderstandings, false accusations, and evil, is doing good. After watching Jesus, Peter learned that it wasn't by slicing off ears that a man overcomes. A man overcomes by quietly trusting God and showing that trust by patiently doing good to the very people that misunderstand him. Whether it is the waitress giving you a hot dog instead of the hamburger you ordered, or an angry official condemning you to jail for being a Christian, you have the opportunity to glorify God by following Jesus' example. Your quiet response, your forgiving attitude, and your continual well doing will reveal God's heart to a lost world and thereby draw people to Him.

At times you might get tired of being misunderstood. You might get weary of doing good things to those who falsely accuse you. Don't lose heart; don't quit. Remember the bigger picture of displaying the nature of God to the world around you, especially in misunderstandings.

For consider Him that endured such contradiction of sinners against Himself lest ye be wearied and faint in your minds (Hebrews 12:3).

Questions

- Name a foolish way to respond to a false accusation.

- Do you think that God ever sets up misunderstandings? Why would He do that?

- Who is the best example of a mature man?

- How does a mature man respond to misunderstandings and false accusations?

The vast majority of men, in all ages and countries, must work before they can eat. Even those who are not under the necessity, are...to adopt what is called an active pursuit of some sort...every member of a community is bound to do something for that community, in return for what he gets from it.

—Earl of Derby to the pupils of
Liverpool College

No Rest Without Work

Let's have fruit for breakfast!" Mom announces. "Great idea," responds Dad. "I'll go get it."

Dad grabs the large silver bowl on the porch and heads out to the orchard. On the way he stops at the young Liberty apple tree in the rabbit pen and puts a few apples in the bowl. Inside the orchard fence he finds a late pear begging to go to breakfast. The Prima apple tree offers four apples. Purple Italian plums join the pile, along with some tight clusters of green seedless grapes. Behind the garden house Dad gently lifts a pear. Without effort it breaks from the branch, declaring itself eligible for picking. A few more apples join the group as Dad returns to the kitchen. A short walk rewards Dad with a harvest of fruit more than enough to feed his family.

This harvest seemed restful, and it was, but it would never have happened without many hours of work. Dad and Mom had bought the ground fourteen years before. They logged a portion large enough to build a house and plant gardens. They bought young trees and dug holes to plant them. They pruned, watered, fertilized, sprayed for worms, and built a fence to keep out the deer. All that is behind them now. Dad picked enough fruit for breakfast and sits at the table eating with his family. Dad rests because he first worked.

God set the example of work before rest when He created the world. He worked six days and then rested on the seventh. He not only set the example, but He made it a law of the universe just as sure as the law of gravity. There is always work before rest. If there is any rest in your life, it is because you or somebody else has worked first.

Shane lays himself down to sleep in an average American home. While lying there he considers the work that others have done to allow him to rest comfortably. "Mom sewed my pajamas. Uncle Peter built my bed. Someone in a factory wove my blankets and made my pillow. My sister washed my sheets. Dad built our house." Shane could continue counting for a long time if he considered all the people who have worked to provide a pleasant community and free country where he can lay his head in peace.

Imagine if Shane found himself dropped into a jungle alone. Could he rest peacefully his first night? Without a refrigerator Shane would have to hunt for food. Without a bed and blankets he might get little sleep, especially when he heard the lions roaring. Life has no rest without previous work. Only as Shane worked very hard could he survive at all, let alone get a good night's sleep.

Many people in America don't rest peacefully in their beds. Part of the reason is that someone has stopped working. Someone has begun to take instead of give. When a society has more takers than givers, that society loses its peacefulness.

In *The Swiss Family Robinson*, the family found themselves shipwrecked on a remote island. They worked hard to get manmade things off the ship before destroying it. The things other people made gave them a measure of rest. Still, it took much labor to build their tree house. Once built, they found rest from the wild animals and the jungle elements. Then they were free to do other tasks besides trying to survive.

After a man has worked, there is some rest. But in time, the value of that work runs out. A man could build a house and afterwards rest, but if he continues to rest and does not fix the window when it breaks, or put on a new roof when it leaks, his house will crumble around him and he will find himself without a place to sleep. It is a man's lot in life to consistently work—only then will he find rest for himself and those under his care.

A boy begins his life with others working for him. His mother goes through labor just to bring him into the world. During his early days he simply sleeps and eats while others work to provide food and a warm place to lie. Boys were not created to remain babies relying on the work of others. Part of becoming a man means choosing to work so that others may rest.

There is a time for a man to rest. It is at the conclusion of a day of work. Be careful not to cultivate the attitude of working so that you can play. Some men see jobs as a way to earn money to buy toys for their day off. Rather, have the attitude that you plan your rest and play so that you may be refreshed to work more.

There is a type of work a man does just to survive. He works for food and shelter. That is the work the Pilgrims did the first winter in America. There is another type of work that helps to make life meaningful for others. It is helping widows, relieving the poor, proclaiming truth. It is using your skills to make this world a better place. When a man has his basic needs met, he can then use his time to be about some good task that will bring rest or relief to others.

George Washington did not have to work each day just to provide for his food and shelter. He could have enjoyed living at Mount Vernon, reaping the benefits of his previous work. However, Washington wanted to help provide rest for all Americans by working to create a free nation. For him it meant years of war and years of politics. Refusing rest, he worked. We still receive benefits today from Washington's labor.

Many parents have worked hard and pass on the rewards of their labors to their children in the form of an inheritance. If the children take the money and spend it on playthings and vacations, they have wasted their parent's

work. A wise son will receive the inheritance with a grateful heart and use it for basic survival or as resources for good works. If the amount is large enough that he no longer has to work for his basic needs, he is free to work for the benefit of his countrymen. A Christian young man should not want to take from his parents' labor and use it on his own pleasures. An inheritance is a gift that he can add to and give to the generation following him.

Do you rest on the works of others, or do you work so others may rest? Our duty to those who have worked before us is to work for those who will come after us.

Let him that stole steal no more: but rather let him labor, working with his hands the thing which is good, that he may have to give to him that needeth (Ephesians 4:28).

Questions

- What work has someone done for you that allows you to rest?

- What is the purpose of rest?

- What job can you do, right now, to give someone else some rest?

- If everyone in your home stopped working, what would happen?

- What would happen to a free country if people stopped working and expected the government to provide for their needs?

Real glory springs from the conquest
of ourselves, and without that the
conqueror is naught but the first slave.

—Samuel Smiles

Overcoming Fear

Have you ever been afraid? From time to time everyone experiences a sudden fear. Even someone who usually isn't afraid of snakes jumps when one drops out of a tree onto their head. Apart from this startling fear, there are specific fears that haunt some people all their lives. Water, heights, dogs, and spiders are examples of things that bring fear to many folks. Some people are rarely afraid; others live in constant fear.

Part of growing into a man is overcoming fears. Overcoming is not necessarily getting rid of fears altogether, but it is learning to succeed in spite of them. Throughout history the great leaders of Israel faced tremendous fears. When God asked Moses to appeal to Pharaoh to let the people of Israel out of Egypt, Moses responded by lamenting, "Who am I? …I am not eloquent…I am slow of speech." God responded: "Certainly I will be with thee…I will be with thy mouth, and teach thee what thou shalt say" (Exodus 3:11,12; 4:10,12).

When Joshua received his commission to lead the Israelites into the Promised Land, God told him: "Be strong and of a good courage; be not afraid, neither be thou dismayed: for the Lord thy God is with thee whither-soever thou goest" (Joshua 1:9). Joshua had seen the great cities and the giants who lived in the hills. The potential for fear abounded. God challenged him to live coura-geously because He Himself would be with him.

Gideon, when told to save Israel from the Midianites, questioned aloud, "...shall I save Israel? ...my family is poor...I am the least in my father's house" (Judges 6:15). Gideon's career was plagued with fear. God's words were the same to him as they were to Moses and Joshua before him, "I will be with thee..." (Judges 6:16).

Fear is common. You will have many opportunities to experience it. A Christian overcomes fear by his awareness of God's presence. Knowing that the Creator of the uni-verse stands with you, attentive to every detail of your need, brings confidence. That confidence gives the courage to obey His orders, even when those orders lead you straight into your fears.

In the early 1970s, we experienced a gasoline shortage on the West Coast. Gas stations closed all over town. Whenever a station had gas, a line of cars extended down the street waiting to get in. Some stations pumped only five dollars' worth into each car. Some sold only to odd or even license plate numbers based on the day of the month. Few offered a fill-up.

In the middle of this shortage, I needed to drive five hundred miles for a friend's wedding. Before leaving town I had to buy gas from three different stations to fill my tank. I planned to stop at every open gas station along the route. After two hours of driving, I found the first one. I drove for almost four hundred miles without find-ing another station with gas to sell. I crossed the Golden Gate Bridge at night with my gas gauge on empty. Signs on the bridge promised a $250 fine to stalled vehicles. My stomach knotted and hurt. Driving in the darkness far from home added to my fear. I didn't know if I should keep driving until my car quit or choose a place to pull off until I could find an open station.

God spoke to my heart as I drove along. "Don't worry; I will meet your need. And if I don't meet your need, you will still have Me."

The reminder of His presence gave me courage. I began singing to Him. My heart overflowed with joy and peace. I drove much farther than I thought possible. When I was well outside the city, on a dark stretch of freeway, my car coughed and died. My tank was out of gas, but my heart was full of joy because of my Father's presence.

"What now?" I asked. It was time to walk. Though quite dark, the night air felt warm. Leaving the car, I proceeded up the nearby exit ramp. At the top of the hill I looked down on the lights of two gas stations! I approached and found both to be open. One gave me a can full of gas, and I walked back to my car. On my return, the attendant generously filled my tank. My mouth fell open when I heard him say, "We are the only stations open for 250 miles in any direction!"

Those stations were out of sight from anywhere along the freeway. For me to find gas, I had to run out exactly where I did. God knew that, and His presence had given me courage to keep driving until my tank was empty.

Last summer, a neighbor of mine fell off his roof, breaking a few bones. He'd been putting the sheathing on his new house so he could get the metal roof installed before the fall rains. But with his injuries he needed six to eight weeks to recover before he could work again. I felt the responsibility to finish the project for him, but I didn't want to do it. Why? I have a fear of heights.

This house had a steep, high roof. The rafters were all in place; I just needed to nail plywood on them. There was something about the dried blood on the deck where the owner hit that added to my uneasiness. My fears remained, but the assurance of God's presence and the understanding that it was His desire for me to finish the roof gave me the confidence to proceed.

As I awoke each morning and remembered that I would be on that roof again, my stomach tightened like a pair of wet swimming trunks being wrung out to dry. I'd wear myself out just thinking about going up that ladder again.

My God continued to lead me. Repeatedly I could hear Him encourage my heart just like He challenged Moses, Joshua, and Gideon. The feeling of fear never left me. In spite of it, I finished the project. Before climbing into my truck to drive away that last day, I stopped and looked up at the roof. Instead of fear, I tasted the joy of overcoming. I don't think the victory would have been as sweet without the battle required to win it.

"I write to you young men because you have over-come…" wrote the aging apostle John. Young men are made to overcome. And every man's life is full of fears, challenges, and obstacles that face him. All are battles waiting to be won. You cannot conquer unless there is an enemy to fight. Every man I know experiences fear. All have challenges in front of them. A man's life is full of battles waiting to be won.

The training grounds for overcoming are the small daily battles of your heart. It involves experiencing fears and going ahead in spite of them. It means feeling dull or lazy and still going out to work. Overcoming means giving the anger, the greed, or the lust in your heart the same treatment as you would a raccoon in your henhouse. The battles will come and the joys of victory follow. Set your face and march straight at your fears and enemies. Nine out of ten will scatter before you reach them. The one remaining will be a genuine war to win. You might lose some battles. If you do, get up again and fight until you win. The Bible commentator Matthew Henry said it well, "Never yield to spiritual enemies. Fight until you get the victory. The war and the victory have a glorious triumph and reward."

Men today receive the courage to fight in the same way as the godly men of old—by experiencing God's presence. His presence keeps the man in the battle until God's victory arrives.

He that overcometh shall inherit all things;
and I will be his God, and he shall be my son
(Revelation 21:7).

Questions

• Do you know anyone who has never been afraid?

• What are some fears you face?

• What calmed the fears of Moses, Joshua, and Gideon?

• If you walk toward your fears, what usually happens?

• How can you increase your awareness of God's presence?

Adversity toughens manhood, and the characteristic of the good or the great man is not that he has been exempt from the evils of life, but that he has surmounted them.

—Patrick Henry

Pain

Four-year-old Mark led the troop of boys and fathers down the gravel road to the creek. In his excitement he began to run. His little legs quickly picked up speed. The two fathers yelled, "Slow down, Mark!" Mark was past the point of slowing down. His legs couldn't keep under his speeding body. Slammmm! skiddddd! Mark acted out a great imitation of a road grader! His brother Stephen helped him up. "Nice slide, Mark!" someone yelled. When Dad got there, he picked him up in a jovial manner. Mark bled a little. He might have felt like crying, but he didn't. All the men bragged about his adventure as being a feat worth rejoicing over. Soon Mark forgot about the slide. I don't think he even noticed the blood. At least he didn't mention it.

Mark is training to be a man. To become a man, in the honorable sense of the word, every boy must learn to face pain head on. It's a part of everyday life. Often it's the small cost of obtaining wisdom, strength, and skill.

A self-centered boy is overly sensitive to pain. He thinks of his own happiness and overrates what makes him feel uncomfortable. He lets pain stop him from his responsibilities. When he should be out working, he thinks about how hot it is. When he should stand and give his chair to a lady who just entered the room, he thinks about how tired he is. He thinks about the scab on his wrist and doesn't want to wash the dishes. There are thousands of opportunities for a selfish boy to think about pain instead of thinking about what he should be doing.

Let's face it. Life hurts. All of creation groans under some sort of pain. Sometimes it is a physical hurt, like Mark's slide on the gravel. Other times it is a hurt in your heart, when someone says something sharp or unkind. Everyone experiences hurt. It is not some special attack upon you! There is no reason to feel sorry for yourself when you hurt, because *every creature hurts*. A man needs to learn how to deal with

pain. If you try to live without pain, you might as well give up and die. A man who hides from pain hides from life.

A few facts about pain help a man endure it. We have already mentioned the first fact. Pain is common to all, so relax, don't see it as unusual. A second fact is that all pain is temporary. Our bodies heal. Smash your finger with a hammer and it hurts. But a year later you probably won't feel a thing. There is no pain in heaven. That means that some day all pain will come to an end. Things that hurt today may not hurt tomorrow. And some things that hurt all your life here will stop hurting there. So don't dwell on your pain—it will pass away.

All pain is limited. Pain is not free to hurt as much as it wants. It is never out of control. Sometimes it feels like the pain is more than we can handle, but it isn't. Pain is controlled by a tender, attentive God who understands our specific limits. He never gives us more than we can endure. When the devil wanted to afflict Job, he had to ask God first. God only allowed as much as he knew Job could handle, and no more. God has the same care for you. He does allow pain, but only within His careful measure and not one ounce more.

All pain is useful. God doesn't create something for no reason at all. You may not understand the reasons for pain, but you can be quite sure that it is good. It is not wise to go looking for pain. However, when it comes, rest in the knowledge that it will work the good it came to accomplish.

Sometimes the hardest pain to endure is pain in our hearts. It is the pain that comes when someone hurts us by what they say or what they do. Maybe it is a misunderstanding or some expectation that didn't get fulfilled. This pain is most intense when it comes from the people close to us, the people we care about most. David lamented, "For it was not an enemy that reproached me; then I could have borne it…But it was thou, a man mine equal, my guide, and mine acquaintance. We took sweet counsel together, and walked unto the house of God in company" (Psalm 55:12-14). When someone says or does something unkind, or even downright mean, your response shows whether you are growing into a man of God or whether you are becoming self-centered and overly sensitive to pain. David responded by crying out to God. There he found comfort.

When faced with pain, many men think only of themselves. You have all watched a boy scream uncontrollably over a small injury. You have seen others get mad if they don't get their way. You have heard complainers whine about being uncomfortable. Many men try to keep away from every type of pain. None of these methods are fitting for a godly man.

When your body is injured, don't be overly concerned about it. If you need stitches or your bones set, go take care of it. But don't show off your bruise to everyone that comes around. A man does not need the sympathy of others. Everybody is injured at some time or another—it is not worth making a scene about it. Instead of occupying your mind with your hurts, be about your responsibilities and help others with theirs.

When your heart is injured, don't get caught up in self-pity. Our Creator's method for responding to pain is to overcome it with good. Don't lie in the corner like a whipped dog, licking your wounds. Step forward and do something good to the very ones that hurt you. If you want a life of adventure, try loving the people that bring you pain. A godly man thinks more about the needs of his enemies than his own feelings.

Learn a lesson from mothers. It is painful to give birth to a child. However, a courageous mom does not concentrate on her pain when delivering a baby; she concentrates on the child to come. She looks past the present, to the wonder of a new life. A man needs this perspective.

Jesus understood pain. "For the joy that was set before him; he endured the cross" (Hebrews 12:2). He kept His focus on all the good that would come from His death. He could see the multitudes of people set free from bondage. He willingly went through intense pain and shame to gain that freedom for them. Let Him be the example of what your attitude should be.

Pain will come. You will hurt. Your usefulness in this world will depend on your willingness to set aside the pain to do all the good you know you should.

> *For I reckon that the sufferings of this present time are not worthy to be compared with the glory which shall be revealed in us*
> (Romans 8:18).

Questions

- Who experiences pain?

- Who controls all pain?

- Have you ever been hurt?

- Did you get over it?

- When a man sees something good that he should do, but knows that it will hurt if he does it, what should he do?

- What is Jesus' attitude toward pain?

- What did David do when his friend hurt him?

Affection does not beget weakness, nor is it effeminate for a brother to be firmly attached to a sister. Such a boy will make a noble and brave man.

—The Golden Gems of Life

Preparing for a Wife

At your age, you might feel funny reading about marriage—especially your own marriage. The topic might make you feel like laughing. That's okay because it probably isn't time for you to get married. Even so, you don't want to miss the chance to learn lessons that will help you should that day come. You can do some things today to prepare for manhood and a happy marriage. It is not that you need to rush into marriage; however, it is better to be ready before the occasion than to struggle in it after you say "I do." If you plan to never marry, the following activity will prepare you to be a gracious bachelor.

God designed perfect classrooms for marriage training. They are called little sisters. Hopefully, you have one or more of these little girls around your home. If you don't happen to have one, an older sister or your mother will do. If you don't have either of those, surely God will provide a substitute for you.

Why is a little sister a good classroom to help prepare you for marriage? Because little sisters love big brothers. Their eyes light up when they see their brothers come into the room. Little sisters are a brother's biggest fan club. If you are going to work on a relationship with someone, it is easiest to begin with someone who already loves you. Little sisters come preprogrammed to love big brothers.

Brothers and sisters that maintain a healthy relationship remain closer than friends throughout life. Your sister is someone who will live or die for you and someone who will help mold your character for good. She is also just the one to teach you how to be a husband, should you ever need to know. Close brothers and sisters think about one another. Their everyday lives show it. A strong sibling relationship shouts to a world full of broken family ties, "Two people, despite faults, can love one another for life!"

The actions that build a good relationship with a sister are the same actions that build a good relationship with a wife. From your sister, you can learn to cultivate good habits that will ensure close relationships as you grow older.

Here are some practical projects that provide training for your future and a joyful home now.

Get to know your sister's desires. What does she like? What does she dislike? Do you know her dreams or her fears? What are her hopes for today and for her tomorrows? Girls do not tell rude and silly boys their hearts' secrets. They do not reveal cherished dreams for careless boys to trample with laughter. The boy who is gentle with his sister is the one to whom she will share her heart. This gentleness is not just a one time thing; it is a way of life. Consistent gentleness is required to gain your sister's trust and open heart. Always be gentle. It is worth repeating— always be gentle.

Once you know the desires of your sister, picture yourself as her personal knight. Accept the challenge of making her dreams come true. Suppose your sister has always wanted to play the violin. Get her one. Pray, work, save, shop.

"Violins are expensive!" you might gasp. "It's too much for a young brother to do for a sister." Yes, it may seem an insurmountable task. That's the idea. A knight doesn't become a knight by doing what any common person can or will attempt to do. Many men have attempted the impossible and—to the surprise of everyone watching—succeeded. Ask God to give you the honor of providing the good things she desires; then work hard. You might be amazed at what you can achieve for your sister if you purpose to do it. Remember, this is a classroom; providing for your sister will educate you to provide for a family in the future. And then in that future, when the road in front of you seems impossible, you can confidently proceed because you remember what God did through you to provide for your sister.

David's confidence to attack Goliath rested upon the days of his youth when he bare-handedly killed a lion and a bear. David told Saul, "The Lord that delivered me out of the paw of the lion, and out of the paw of the bear, he will deliver me out of the hand of this Philistine" (1 Samuel 17:37). If David had not gone out against the lion and bear would he have had the courage to fight Goliath? Take on some challenges in your youth for the sake of your sister and you'll have the confidence to fight for your wife and little ones when you are older.

Another practical project is to understand your sister's fears. Never tease nor belittle her with them. As much as is in your power, give her an environment free from these fears. This is your privilege as a brother.

Instead of competing with your sister to be the strongest or the smartest, see yourselves on the same team. Help her reach her full potential. Instead of gloating over being faster, train her to run. Be her coach instead of her opponent.

Develop thoughtfulness by practicing on your sister. Let her have the biggest piece of pie, or the best seat in the car. Treat her with courtesy. Open the door for her. Find her coat. Introduce her to your friends. When she does well, praise her. When her faults show, forgive her and cover them.

Though you are not the only influence in your sister's life, God can use you to give her hope and courage. You have the opportunity to help her become a beautiful lady inside and out. Have you considered asking your sister to read the Bible with you? Do you pray with her, just the two of you? If you are consistent to love your sister today, she will say when she is older, "My brother made a huge

difference in my life. He helped me reach my dreams. I love him and respect him."

You might be saying, "This won't work. My sister doesn't like me!" The answer to your statement might sound stern, but it is true. You are selfish. Quit thinking about you. Think about her. She likes you more than you know. Even if you are right and she doesn't like you, she did once. If you have one of those unhealthy relationships, don't worry how you got there. Get out of it. Accept the situation as a classroom; your homework assignment is to restore the relationship. If she liked you once, she could again.

Whether your sister likes you or not, the issue is taking care of her. Sure, it is easier if she likes you, but that isn't a requirement. God takes care of millions of people who don't like Him at all. He desires that you do the same. A mature man is not concerned with who likes him and who doesn't. He sets a course of well doing, regardless of the response.

"What if my sister blows up at me and says she doesn't like all the attention?" you ask. Don't believe her, she likes attention. She might not like the way you are giving it. The way a boy likes to do something is not always the way a girl likes it. Also, what a girl likes one day, she may not like the next. That is part of the challenge of learning to love a sister. Ask your mom to suggest things you might do differently. It's a man's job to learn how a girl likes things, and then to creatively proceed on her terms.

These are just a few ideas about how to cherish and nurture your sister. Of course, there are many more practical things a boy can do. The main lesson is: learn how to think about somebody other than yourself. Your sister provides the perfect opportunity for practice. As you grow in your love for her, you will become educated in how to love a wife, should you find one some day.

Whoso findeth a wife findeth a good thing and obtaineth favor of the Lord (Proverbs 18:22).

Questions

• Name a classroom where a boy might learn about marriage.

• If your sister doesn't like you, what is the usual reason?

• What quality in a boy tends to make his sister want to share her heart with him?

• Name one practical project you can do to develop a closer relationship with your sister.

The Bible is the Word of life—it is a picture of the human heart displayed for all ages and all sorts of conditions of men. I feel sorry for the men who do not read the Bible every day. I wonder why they deprive themselves of the strength and pleasure.

—Woodrow Wilson

The Best Book

George Cox—just to look at him you wouldn't see anything special. He wasn't tall. He wore glasses. Two of his fingers were lost in a mill accident. He looked down as he spoke in his quiet manner. The other guys his age often teased him.

It was George that came alongside me as I walked on the beach one morning. I had committed my life to Christ the night before. He wanted to share some practical lessons with me. I was fifteen, George was about twenty. "It's real important," he began, "when a guy becomes a Christian that he meets regularly with someone older than himself. Many fellows around here would be willing to take you under their wing." He named a few men I knew and then continued, "I also would be glad to meet weekly with you and teach you what others have taught me. Think about it. But, be sure that you meet with someone."

I didn't know George well, but I asked him to teach me the basics of Christianity. He said he would. For the next two years, George and I met weekly. The lessons he shared changed my life.

"You can always tell if a person has made a genuine commitment to Christ," George said, "by their hunger for the Bible." He challenged me to read it every day and checked on my progress each week. George taught me a simple way to study the Bible. After reading a portion I would answer two questions in a notebook. First, what does the passage say? Second, because of what it says, what do I need to change in my thoughts or actions to align with that truth? He inspired me to memorize the sixty verses from the Navigator's Topical Memory System. He showed me how to meditate on those verses. Best of all, he encouraged me to live what the Bible taught. George gave to me his love for the greatest book in the world.

If your mom gave you a white shirt to wear on special occasions, and you used it to clean the rims on your bicycle, how useful would it be the next time you wanted to dress up for a wedding? In the same way, many boys damage their lives by doing things they were never intended to do.

The Bible explains how to use your life. It describes how to get along with anyone you ever meet. Parents, brothers and sisters, friends, enemies, employers, girls, older folks, and babies are all covered. It tells you how to drive, how to work, and how to invest your money for the greatest return. It warns of the people who want to trap you. It tells you when to eat and when to sleep. The Bible contains the principles governing every area of life.

The Bible does much more than teach principles. This book describes the person of God and how to hear His voice. It allows you to see life from His perspective. The Bible gives insight into the nature of the grandest Being in the universe.

Jesus Christ is the visible expression of the God we cannot see with our eyes. As you read about Jesus, you grow in your understanding of God as our Father. From Genesis to Revelation, the life of Jesus is carefully described. No important information is omitted. Through Jesus, a man may receive the greatest of all gifts—eternal life in the presence of God the Father. It is the Bible that tells us so.

You are not just an animal. You were created with a spirit that has deep inner questions. Every man comes to the place where he wants answers to these questions. Where did I come from? What happens when I die? Why is there pain and suffering? The Bible holds the answers.

What book do you own that offers more than this? One hour in any other book cannot compare to one hour in the Bible.

"When you say it like that, it makes sense," I hear a reader lament, "but the Bible is dull to me. I don't get excited about reading the Bible like I do other books." You are not the first to admit those feelings. One reason that the Bible is dull to many people is that they don't set out to live it. The Bible is a book to be lived, not simply read.

How can you increase your interest in the Bible? Live what you read. Suppose you read in Matthew 5 the words of Jesus, "Love your enemies, bless them that curse you, do good to them that hate you, and pray for them which despitefully use you, and persecute you." This is practical instruction for interacting with people who are at odds with you. Ask God to live this truth through you and then do it.

Perhaps your neighbor, Mr. Riley, is a grouchy fellow. You are sure that he doesn't like you. He yells at your dog every time she goes into his yard. Here is a good candidate for applying that verse. Begin by giving him a blessing. If you see him working in his yard, call to him over the fence, "May your garden give you a great harvest this year, Mr. Riley!" Look for needs. When it snows, shovel his walk. When the wind breaks a large limb out of his tree, help him clean it up. Pray for him. "God, would You give Mr. Riley the ability to see the sunny side of life?"

When you follow the Bible's advice, it becomes real to you. Your actions will bring a change to your heart, and it may bring a change to Mr. Riley's. Keep doing what you read, and you will want to know all that is in this great book.

It is not the scholar who sits in his room having devotions and debating Bible truths who really understands it. The men who read it, believe it, and live it are the ones with understanding. The Bible is not just a book with pleasant stories. It is a book to live.

If you read the Bible for five minutes every day as some sort of devotion, and then live contrary to what you read, the book will be very dull. You will be a man who builds the house of his life on the sand. The floods will come and your house will fall. But if you read even only one sentence a day and live it, you will be a man whose life is built on a solid foundation.

Anything a man does not understand will become dull. In some parts of the Bible, finding anything practical is a challenge. Don't feel bad about leaving those sections until a later day when your understanding increases or when someone can help you. It is far better to concentrate on reading and doing what you understand than to spend hours trying to appreciate something that doesn't make sense. Read Mark's fast-moving account of the life of Jesus, or the practical instruction of Proverbs, rather than wading through Moses' account of building the tabernacle. The day will come when you will see how the tabernacle is a clear picture of the life of Christ, and it will encourage you. But in the meantime, read and live what you understand.

Thirty-five years ago, George began challenging me to read my Bible. Today he continues to read and live it. His encouragement and example changed my life. I hope you will read your Bible every day of your life. And more importantly, may you continually live what you read.

> *And that from a child thou hast known the holy scriptures, which are able to make thee wise unto salvation through faith which is in Christ Jesus. All scripture is given by inspiration of God, and is profitable for doctrine, for reproof, for correction, for instruction in righteousness: That the man of God may be perfect, thoroughly furnished unto all good works* (2 Timothy 3:15-17).

One More Thing

The Bible gives a boy the reason to learn to read better. Reading the Bible with your own eyes is worth all the effort required to learn. Perhaps you are a poor reader; you may even feel like a failure. You don't have to remain that way. If you set your mind and work at it every day, you will become a good reader. Don't learn to read because your teacher or your parents want you to. Learn to read because you want to. Don't be in a hurry. With steady careful effort you will improve and you will learn about life. Be a good reader for your own benefit, that the advantages of the Bible may be yours for a lifetime.

Questions

• What did George say was one mark of a genuine Christian?

• What are two reasons why the Bible may seem dull?

• The Bible is very practical. How can the following verse apply to driving? "Wine is a mocker, strong drink is raging: and whosoever is deceived thereby is not wise" (Proverbs 20:1).

• What is more important, reading the Bible or living it? Why?

Avail yourself of the greatest privilege this side of heaven. Jesus Christ died to make this communion and communication with the Father possible.

—Billy Graham

The Morning Watch

Jared wants to start meeting with God in the mornings. After turning off the alarm, he grabs a Bible, curls up in the blankets to keep warm, and turns to the first page of the New Testament.

He begins reading in Matthew, chapter one: "The book of the generation of Jesus Christ, the son of David, the son of Abraham. Abraham begat Isaac; and Isaac begat Jacob; and Jacob begat Judas and his brethren; and Judas begat Phares and Zara of Thamar…" Jared lowers his head until it rests lightly on the pillow.

He continues reading, "…and Phares begat Esrom; and Esrom begat Aram; And Aram begat Aminadab; and…zzzzzzzzzzzz."

"It's time to get up, son," Father says, gently shaking Jared's shoulder. "Breakfast is ready."

"Good morning, Dad. I'll be right down."

At breakfast, Jared confided in his father, "I want to meet with God in the mornings, but I don't know what to do. I tried this morning. I fell asleep almost as soon as I got started. What do you do, Dad? Do you have any tips for me?"

"I'm not an expert on the topic, but I can tell you what I do. Let's go for a walk after we eat and talk about it."

Passing through the utility room, they grabbed their coats and hats before heading out the door. For a few minutes they walked, silently enjoying the crisp morning.

"Jared," began Dad. "The first thing about getting up early in the morning is simple; go to bed early at night."

"How do you know what's early?" asked Jared.

"Early in the morning is getting up before you *have to* so that you can spend a relaxed time with God before the day starts. Early at night is going to bed so that you can get up refreshed at your early in the morning time. My biggest hindrance to getting up early is getting to bed late."

"You're up pretty late sometimes when we have company," said Jared.

"Occasionally it's necessary to stay up. However, a general rule of going to bed early is the first step toward getting up in the morning."

Dad continued, "I can fall asleep in less than a minute if given the chance, especially in the morning. I have to get out of bed quickly or I'm asleep again. At night, before I crawl into bed, I lay out my clothes for the next day. I set my shoes by my door. My glasses are on the dresser where I can find them even in the dark. Everything is in a line between my bed and where I will meet with God."

"That's real organized, Dad. I didn't know you did that."

"It's not that I'm trying to be organized. It is just that I know myself. If I lie in bed deciding what to wear, I'll fall asleep. I avoid all decisions until I'm up, dressed, and ready for the day."

"What do you do then, Dad?"

"My morning times have changed through the years. But I remember clearly how they started. A friend gave me a booklet called *7 minutes with God*. It described 'The Morning Watch,' something very simple. It challenged me to set aside seven minutes every morning to meet with God."

"Only seven minutes! That's not very long," said Jared.

"You're right, that's not long, but it's a start. Most great things in life start small. Often the boy who looks down on little things because he wants to accomplish great things never completes either."

"But what do you do in seven minutes?"

"According to the booklet, the first thirty seconds are set aside to prepare your heart by greeting God and yielding yourself to Him. The next four minutes are for Bible reading. The last two and a half minutes are for prayer. They divide the prayer time into four particular types of prayers: praise, confession, thanksgiving, and praying for the needs of others and yourself.

"I liked how simple it was. I knew what to do first. And I knew when I was done. I rarely finished within seven minutes; I think that was their idea. Early rising to meet God became a lifelong habit for me, but as the booklet warned, 'Do not become devoted to a habit, but to the Savior.'"

"Do you still follow the seven-minute plan?" asked Jared.

Dad looked down the road as he thought about the question. He chuckled to himself and then answered "I almost said no. But, as I consider it, I still do. I begin with prayer, end with prayer and my in-between time is centered in the Word."

"What do you do in-between?"

"The goal of my morning is to gain an understanding of God's heart and to share my heart with Him. Everything I do works toward that end. I almost always have a bookmark in my Bible where I left off reading one day and where I plan to start the next. What I do after that varies considerably.

"Sometimes I slowly read until one idea touches my conscience. While reading 'Blessed are the peacemakers...' I might recall a situation when I wasn't a peacemaker. At that point, I stop and pray. I confess my sin and purpose to change. If what I read prompts me to a particular action, like peacemaking, that might be all the reading I need for the day.

"Do you remember the year I wanted to know what God thought about families? I started in Genesis and read through Revelation, keeping a notebook of insights. I know now why God calls Himself 'Father.'

"I've studied books of the Bible, word by word, using a dictionary to help me understand the meaning. I've studied people, the events of Jesus' life, and the attributes of God. Right now I'm reading in the Gospels."

"I tried Matthew this morning," interrupted Jared. "It was boring. I fell sleep before I finished the first chapter. It was just one name after another."

"I often skip the lists of names," laughed Dad.

"Don't you feel guilty?" asked Jared.

"No."

"Aren't you supposed to read straight through?" he questioned.

"Jared, there are no rules like that when it comes to reading the Bible. I skip the genealogies when reading them becomes a religious exercise. If I read them only so that I can say I read that chapter, I've missed the point of the Bible. The purpose of the Bible is to draw us into a relationship with God, not to provide us with a religious endurance test.

"It's not to say that the genealogies aren't useful. I've gone through every list of names in the Bible looking up their definitions one by one. Just reading the meanings of those names in their order tells the Gospel of Jesus Christ. It's a great project, but on other days I might skip them.

"Jared, I say this because it is possible to worship the Bible in place of worshipping God. The Bible is the Book of all books, inspired by God Himself. I cannot speak highly enough of its worth. However, as men in the Bible were warned not to worship angels, who brought the messages of God, we are not to worship the Bible.

Therefore, use it for the tool it is, to display God, not as a slave master."

"That's a relief when you say it like that, Dad. This morning's reading was too much for me.

"Do you do anything else in the mornings?" asked Jared.

"Often I'll record the lessons I learn in a journal. I also write down things I need to change in my life. Sometimes God prompts me to take the morning lesson and write it in a letter to a friend. In the summer, I go for walks in the woods. In the winter I might sit by the fire. Occasionally I will sing or pace the room quoting verses. And when tired of activities, I might follow His leading to be still and know that He is God."

"Dad, God's not as real to me as He is to you."

"That's the reason why you want to spend every possible morning with Him. You'll grow as you read His Word and pray to Him. He will speak to you. He promises in John 14:21 to make Himself known to you as you keep His words.

"Try again tomorrow," encouraged Dad. "Don't give up. 'The Morning Watch' is a basic part of the greatest adventure in life—walking with God."

As they took off their coats in the utility room, Jared turned to his dad and said, "Thanks for the walk; I won't give up."

And in the morning, rising up a
great while before day, he [Jesus] went out,
and departed into a solitary place,
and there prayed (Mark 1:35).

Questions

- Why did Dad get everything ready the night before?

- Why did Jared fall asleep trying to read his Bible?

- What methods did Dad use to learn about God from the Bible?

- Do you have a morning watch with God?

Associate yourself with men of good quality.

—George Washington

The Value of an Old Man

Timmberrrrrrrrrrrrr! In the forests of the McKenzie Valley, Wilburn Poff and Don Thienes harvested trees for lumber and paper.

Wilburn was born in Mountain View, Arkansas in 1915. In 1950 he moved to Oregon, and after six months began logging. Wilby, as the men called him, moved at one speed: steady. With calm purpose he thoughtfully went about his business and his life.

Don was born three years after Wilby had started in the woods. Eighteen years later they teamed up to work together. Thienes was young, strong, and fast. He showed up to work not to put in his hours but to turn trees into logs. He hustled and tried to get old Wilby to speed up.

"Donald," Wilby would say, "the faster I go, the behinder I get."

Like most young men, Don thought that if he could just put out a little more speed, he would accomplish more. Wilby wasn't convinced.

With a deep respect and love for one another, they cut and bucked side by side, each in his own way. Don worked fast but he couldn't keep ahead of slow and steady Wilby. At times, it took all Don's strength to get out of the trouble his speed got him into.

The secret to Wilby's success was that he didn't make mistakes. His steady pace and clear thinking allowed him to successfully compete with the strength and speed of youth. For nearly thirty years, until he retired at age sixty-five, Wilby worked his dangerous job without a serious accident. He finished as productive as he started.

When Don became irritated by the heat of the summer or the cold of the winter, old Wilby would speak, not straight at Don, but as if to a nearby tree:

> As a rule a man's a fool,
> When it's hot, he wants it cool,
> When it's cool, he wants it hot,
> Always wanting what it's not.

Wilby had watched the seasons come and go many times. He knew that winter would be here before you knew it. He understood the power of patience.

Though young, Don saw the worth of the old man's life and advice. It's been twenty-seven years now since the two of them worked together. Don's life continues to prove the truth of Wilburn Poff's perspective. It's not strength and speed but slow and steady that wins the race.

Often boys are unable to see the value of old men. *What does that old man know?* they think to themselves. *I can outlift him and outrun him. His ways are old-fashioned, and he doesn't understand today's world.* A young fool's perspective of age is "old, slow, and unproductive."

It's hard for a young man to be wise, because he hasn't lived long enough to see the results of his actions. An old man has experienced the rewards of hard work and the consequences of slothfulness. He has watched the results of hurry and the fruit of steady effort. Seasons have come and gone, and the old man knows the benefits of each. He enjoys what is at hand while patiently waiting for the benefits of the seasons to come.

Age and experience bring wisdom. When nearing twenty-five, you begin to understand what you should have done at fifteen. At thirty, you see the value of the character your parents tried to instill in you years before. At fifty, you learn how you should have acted at thirty. When you're young, life is a theory. When you are older it has become an experience.

It's wise to ask men who are ten to twenty years older than yourself how they would live if they were your age. Most will gladly relate their mistakes and victories, if you're willing to listen. It doesn't matter if the man is an honorable person or one who has made shambles of his life. The lessons from both are profitable.

When I began to frame houses, I used a thirty-two-ounce hammer. All the young guys used them. A thirty-two-ounce hammer is heavy, but once you get it in the air, it drives a nail with one stroke. I changed jobs and began working with older men. The old fellows told me, "Use a smaller hammer. You'll wear out your arm!" I was convinced they said that only because they weren't strong enough to lift my hammer.

I'm older now. I damaged my right arm using that big hammer, and it has never completely healed. I drive my truck with my left arm because it hurts to use my right one. What did those old fellows know anyway?

When I was twenty-two, if a young man asked me what size hammer he should use, I would tell him, "If you are man enough, use a thirty-two-ounce." But now, because I have seen the fruit and the consequences, I'd smile and say, "Use a sixteen- to twenty-two-ounce hammer; or you might ruin your arm."

A boy who listens to an older man, like his father, and follows his advice, will not look like the other boys his age. He'll seem a little odd, maybe a little too conservative. He'll think about the end result instead of just plowing ahead with any idea that tumbles into his mind. He's the one who keeps his friends out of trouble by saying, "My dad wouldn't do that, let's pick something else." Respectable people will comment, "That young man is mature for his age."

After the death of King Solomon, his son Rehoboam went to the town of Shechem to receive his kingship. The people of Israel asked him to make their yoke lighter and they would remain faithful servants. Rehoboam asked the old men how he should respond to this request. They counseled him to be kind to the people and to please them. If he did so, the old men assured, all Israel would serve him.

Next, Rehoboam asked the young men what they thought he should do. They counseled him to be more dominating than his father. Rehoboam decided to follow the young men's advice. He told the people, "My father made your yoke heavy, and I will add to your yoke: my father also chastised you with whips, but I will chastise you with scorpions" (1 Kings 12). Ten out of the twelve tribes in Israel rebelled against Rehoboam after he spoke these words.

What is the value of an old man? For Rehoboam, listening to the old men could have saved his kingdom. For you, an old man's experience, his failures and victories, might help you avoid foolish mistakes. He is like a road map that tells you where a particular road leads, *before* you choose to go down it. An old man is an encyclopedia of firsthand experiences, a history book, a landmark, and a treasure chest of facts and skills. Old men are priceless gifts to the boys who are wise enough to open them.

Many old men do not talk readily. They often just watch. Inwardly they evaluate the boys around them. *This one will make it. If that one keeps doing what he is doing, he won't.* Years of experience often prove their judgment correct.

Don't count on men offering you advice, even when they see you about to make a big mistake. Their advice has been rejected many times. They may just keep quiet, rather than make waves, or enemies, by speaking up.

It's the young man's responsibility to draw out the old man's advice. Finding men like Wilburn Poff, and investing the time required to draw out his wisdom, is one of the best investments for the future a boy can make.

O God, thou hast taught me from my youth:
and hitherto have I declared thy wondrous
works. Now also when I am old and gray-
headed, O God, forsake me not; until I have
shown thy strength unto this generation,
and thy power to everyone that is to come
(Psalm 71:17,18).

Questions

• Why was the old cutter able to accomplish as much or more than the young, strong cutter?

• How did the old carpenters know that a large hammer could ruin a man's arm?

• Why didn't the young carpenter change hammers after being warned?

• Why did Rehoboam lose most of his kingdom?

• What is the value of an old man?

A young man may gain a wealth of information from older men. Here is a sample of questions you might ask.

You won't be able to run down the list and get one great answer after another. It takes time. You may need to simply ask an older man about a job he had, or his family, and just let him take the conversation where his memory leads. If you are alert and willing to spend the time, you'll gather gems of wisdom.

Questions for an Interview with an Older Man

1. What profitable investments have you made? What investments didn't turn out so well? (These could be money investments or investments in time, skills, relationships, etc.)
2. What things do you wish you had studied? What skills do you wish you had developed?
3. Do you have any tips for maintaining good relationships? Did you ever have a relationship damaged by misunderstandings that were never cleared up?
4. What were the best times of your life?
5. How have you seen our society change? For the better? For the worse?
6. What lessons can you teach me about marriage? About children?
7. If you were a boss for a company, what would you look for in an employee?
8. When you were a young man, do you remember any advice your father or an older man gave you? Did you follow it?
9. What things are most important to you at this time in your life?
10. Do you feel ready to die?

I want to see my sons strong...
to work, hunt, and to provide for
themselves and others, and to
fight if necessary.

—Johann David Wyss,
The Swiss Family Robinson

A Time to Kill

There is a time to kill. One challenge of growing into a man is learning when it is time to kill and when it is not. Sometimes people get mixed up and kill when they shouldn't and refuse to kill when they should. How can a boy know when it is right?

Man is not just another animal. He was given dominion over the earth and over all other animals. Men and women are created by God to exercise authority over all living things. They are responsible to treat all nature with respect and honor because nature is a reflection of God. Man's dominion over the animals gives him the right to use them to benefit himself, his family, and his community. But he is never to be cruel to any.

A boy can ask two questions to know if his intent to kill is just or not. What am I protecting? And for what am I providing? His answers will help direct his actions.

When the carpenter ants moved into the floor under the shower, it was time to kill. They don't belong under the shower, destroying the floor. To protect the bathroom, the ants had to go. With some persuading they did. If I was walking in the woods and saw a nest of carpenter ants working over an old stump, it would be cruel to kill them. One purpose of a carpenter ant is to turn rotting wood into dust. In the woods they are justified in their actions. In my bathroom they are not.

To provide chemical-free food for our table, we ordered fifty chickens. After seven weeks of caring for their welfare by kindly providing food, water, and shelter, it was a time to kill. I never grew up killing animals to eat. I ate my share, but someone else always killed and packaged them for me. It was my turn to kill. I have killed many chickens since, but never without a feeling of respect and appreciation for their life that allows me to live. Their blood is always a sober reminder of Jesus, who willingly shed His blood for me. Tomorrow we will be canning tuna. Again, the purpose of this killing is to supply food for my family throughout the year.

It is a man's role to provide a peaceful place to rear his family. At times, it requires killing to achieve that purpose. Bats decided to live on our house. On the dark porch, they often screamed while our family entered the front door. They left their wastes on the rails. Some even crawled around on the walls in broad daylight. You should have heard the screams when one of them flew around in the living room! When the bats took over our front porch, the garden house, and came into our living room, it became time to kill.

I didn't kill for the fun of it. I didn't kill out of anger. I killed to protect and to provide.

I killed to protect my family from the diseases these creatures carried. My neighbor contracted rabies from a bat bite. The bat was not being malicious. He simply fell on my neighbor and bit him in the excitement. I killed to provide a restful place for my family to dwell.

I don't enjoy killing, but it is a necessary part of being a man. Plenty of bats still fly around the yard at night. But they don't live with my family.

There are some godly men who have fought in wars to protect our homes and to provide freedom for our families and communities. Some have taken up arms to protect their homes from evil men that wanted to kill and destroy. Their motive is a God-given drive to protect and provide.

Other godly men, for the sake of their consciences, will not take up arms against another man. These men see that their role is to honor the life of other humans because they are made in the image of God. These men purpose to never kill. Both perspectives have at their roots the desire to live in a peaceful state. Both need to be clear in their minds if it is time to exercise force to protect those given to their charge. Both still have the responsibility to protect and provide though they may choose different paths to that end.

When I was in high school, some of my friends invited me to go to the woods for the day. They brought along their guns to hunt "diggers." I fired six shots and hit six ground squirrels, killing them all instantly. I laid down the gun. There was no purpose for it. I wasn't protecting anything and I wasn't providing anything. I was just wasting life.

As a man, I am responsible to oversee the creatures that live around me. To kill needlessly is the work of a destroyer, not a protector. Maybe you have killed creatures for no reason. Maybe you have shot at birds just to do it or tortured creatures for the fun of it. Think before you kill. A life is sacred. A man is responsible to protect and provide for the animals and people under his care. Don't kill without a reason. And don't be afraid to kill when it is time to protect or provide.

We live in a day when people will kill their own babies yet won't kill a diseased mouse in their pantry. We are in need of men who have eyes to see the worth of human life. We need men who see the value of animals. We need men who have the courage to kill when it is time to kill.

To everything there is a season. And a time
to every purpose under the heaven:
...A time to kill (Ecclesiastes 3:1,3).

Questions

- When is it time to kill?

- What is man's relationship to animals? (Genesis 1:26; 9:2,3)

- How does a good man treat his animals?

- What should a man provide for his family?

- What should a man protect?

True Devotion does not consist in the performance of certain Religious Duties at set times, but in the Spirit in which the Ordinary Duties of common life are performed.

—William Law,
A Serious Call to a Devout and Holy Life

Worship

Wake up, Paul. I called you almost an hour ago. It's past time to get ready for church. Hurry up. Let's get going." There was a touch of irritation in Mother's voice that set Paul on edge.

"Alright, alright, I'm coming," Paul answered in a less than respectful tone.

In his mind, he carried on a one-sided conversation with his mother. *You don't have to nag at me. I know how long it takes to get ready. Besides, you won't have breakfast ready by the time I get out there. My sister is always later than I am. Why don't you yell at her?*

Paul kicked the cat as he walked down the hall to the bathroom. His sister, still curling her hair, wasn't about to come out.

"Hurry up in there," he barked. "What is taking you so long?"

The oatmeal wasn't hot enough for him. He complained about the shirt he had to wear. In the car, Paul began to gripe about having to sit in the back seat. Father sternly reproved him. Turning his face to the window, Paul pouted all the way to the church.

Slamming the car door, Paul ran to the church steps. His pout turned into a smile. He cheerfully greeted his friends and walked with them to the Sunday school classroom. Today was Paul's turn to lead worship in the youth church. He really liked singing and was good at it. In front of his friends, he sang energetically. Between songs, he challenged the group to "worship with your whole heart."

Paul continued through the Sunday morning routine, attending the main service and doing all that was expected of him. Around twelve o'clock, the family climbed back into the car and drove home.

Paul didn't like the bean soup Mother fixed for lunch. He told her so. Why couldn't she fix hamburgers, like Tony's mom?

The rest of the afternoon, while some took naps, Paul retired to his bedroom and played Space Attack on his computer until it was time to return for the evening service. He looked forward to the night service because the worship time was a real spiritual high for him.

Paul's attitude toward life and worship is not new. Three thousand years ago the nation of Israel prided themselves in their worship meetings. They sacrificed animals just like God said to. They burned incense, sprinkled blood, and met on new moons and Sabbaths. Their solemn services with many prayers and uplifted hands were quite impressive! However, their lives reeked with selfishness.

God spoke through Isaiah to Israel, "Hear the word of the Lord, ye rulers of Sodom; give ear unto the law of our God, ye people of Gomorrah…what purpose is the multitude of your sacrifices unto me?…I am full of burnt offerings…I delight not in the blood of bullocks, or of lambs, or of goats…incense is an abomination unto me;…the calling of assemblies…it is iniquity, even the solemn meeting. And when ye spread forth your hands, I will hide mine eyes from you: yea, when ye make many prayers, I will not hear: your hands are full of blood" (Isaiah 1:10-15).

Originally, God had designed the structure of Israel's worship services. But He became sick of those services because the daily lives of the people were full of wickedness. Worship, for Israel, was not the expression of righteous living that God intended. It changed into an outward show. It was as if Israel had found a dead cat beside the road, scooped it up onto a silver plate, covered it with delicious white frosting, and served it to God as a dessert. Israel thought they were the best worshippers on the face of the earth. In today's language, "they really got into it." God, on the other hand, was repulsed. He hated to see them coming!

After reproving Israel, Isaiah declared God's idea of worship, "Wash you, make you clean; put away the evil of your doings from before mine eyes; cease to do evil; Learn to do well; seek judgment, relieve the oppressed, judge the fatherless, plead for the widow" (Isaiah 1:16,17). To God, justice and judgment are the basis of worship.

Today when we talk about worshipping, we often think about a meeting, or the part of a meeting, where everyone sings. This is far from what God intended. Jesus taught about worshipping in spirit and truth, but never described a meeting. Worship, according to Jesus, was living everyday life by God's standards of justice.

If God sees worship as the way we live, rather than what we do in meetings, what does He think about Paul's worship? Paul may be a good singer, but the worship of his life stinks. If the whole church service were made up of folks like Paul, according to Isaiah, God would not show up!

Paul needs a change of heart. He needs to repent of his selfish ways. And as John the Baptist said, "Bring forth therefore fruits worthy of repentance…" (Luke 1:8). For Paul, those fruits would be things like kindness to his sister, honor to his parents, gratefulness for food regardless of what it is, and contentment with the back seat. The fruit of repentance is a life of justice.

If Paul truly worshipped God, Sunday mornings at Paul's house would look different. Here is a possible rerun:

"Paul, it's time to get up!" calls Mother.

"Thanks, Mom. I'm on my way." Paul springs out of bed, eager for another day to live. Pausing at his window, his heart overflows to God, "Thank you, Lord, for giving me life. You are a great God! Please use me to honor You today."

Dressing quickly, he heads down the hall. His sister is still brushing her hair so Paul continues on to the kitchen.

"Mom, do you need any help?"

"You could set the table," she answers.

Just as Paul finishes the table, his sister appears.

"Hi, Sis. You look great this morning."

After a pleasant ride to the church building, Paul climbs the steps. He prays, "How can I best honor You, Lord?" Paul doesn't have the desire to be up in the front today. Instead he considers the needs of others and does what he can to help.

At home, the lunch is simple and Paul feels grateful to eat it. He cheerfully helps with cleanup and looks forward to the afternoon. In his free time, he plans to read through the Gospel of Mark. It will take a while, but he really wants to hear again the things that Jesus did.

Later, he hopes to visit Mrs. Warner down the street. Her husband died last year. She has twin boys, five years old. When he can, Paul visits and plays games with the boys. Before he leaves, he always tells them a simple Bible story. They love it.

There you have two different stories about Paul. Which one best describes you? The first Paul thought he was worshipping God when he really wasn't. The second Paul worships God by the way he lives.

Men can fool one another when they only interact in religious meetings. It is in business, at home, and in recreation where a man's worship is shown for what it is. God is never fooled. He knows who is worshipping Him and who isn't.

If you want to be the man who lives up to his highest calling of manhood, if you want that privileged position of displaying the nature of God to the world, learn to worship Him the way He wants to be worshipped.

Don't wait for a special meeting; worship God with your life, each moment of the day.

...Worship the Lord in the beauty of holiness
(1 Chronicles 16:29).

Questions

- In the first story, was Paul worshipping God? Why did he think that he was?

- Why did God reject Israel's worship when they were meeting according to His design?

- How often should we worship God?

- Do you remember what William Law said in the quote at the beginning of this chapter?

*A good personal letter can help build
or keep a valuable friendship.*

—World Book Encyclopedia

Letters

Dear Todd,
Building that rock wall for Mr. Hansen yesterday pushed me to my limits. Your example challenged me to work harder than I thought I could. You never complained about the heat. You never asked about the time. And you never stopped working! It is a privilege to be on the same crew with you. My Dad says that someone who works like you will do well in life. I hope that I can learn to be as good a worker as you are.
With much respect,
Roger

Roger wrote this letter to Todd the night after they worked together. Both boys live within two miles of each other. Roger could have just complimented Todd the next time he saw him, or written a few lines by E-mail, or telephoned and told him. All three of those options are good things to do. But in this case Roger chose to send a letter.

Two days later, Todd's little sister Mary ran down the driveway to the house waving a letter over her head.

"It's a letter! It's a letter for you, Todd!" she cried. "Hurry, open it, what does it say!" Mary jumped up and down in front of Todd, eager to learn why he should get a personal letter. The only time they got letters was on their birthdays or occasionally from Grandma. But this was a real letter, and it had Todd's name on it.

Todd read the letter quietly to himself. Mary sat still as a mouse waiting to hear the news.

"Oh, please tell me," she begged once more. Slightly embarrassed, Todd read Roger's praise report of the previous day. Mary, who always thought Todd was the greatest big brother in the world, was sure of it now. "You are a good worker and you should get an award," bragged Mary.

Running into the kitchen, Mary exclaimed, "Todd got a real letter and it tells about what a good worker he is!"

"What is this, Todd?" asked Mom.

"Well, it's just a note from Roger about working on that rock wall the other day," said Todd.

"May I read it?" she inquired.

Todd sheepishly handed over the unfolded page. After a few moments of silent reading, Mom said, "What a thoughtful boy that Roger is! And when your dad reads this, he is going to be a proud father."

As soon as Dad came in the door, Mary danced around him trying to be the first to tell the news of the letter. Mom beamed, and Todd sort of hung his head in the way that says, "Aw, shucks, it's nothin'."

Mary produced the letter, and all were silent while Dad read it over. He looked up, took a step toward Todd, and stuck out his hand.

"Let me shake the hand of a good working man," announced Dad. "I knew you were a hard worker, but to see it here in writing makes my heart extra glad! Thanks for being an honor to the family. You are going to be a useful man in this world, son. Keep it up!"

"Dinner's ready," called Mom.

"We're coming," answered Dad.

Look what a simple hundred-word letter accomplished. If you want to be a man that spreads joy, encouragement, and hope, learn to write simple letters, and then write them. It doesn't matter if your spelling is exact. Maybe your penmanship lacks a little style. If you write letters, both of those small troubles will begin to disappear.

A letter of encouragement is easy to write. First, look around you at the everyday people in your life. What do

they do that is good? How do they benefit your life or the lives of others? When you see something, write it down, along with how much you appreciated what it was they did. Address the envelope, put a stamp on it, and stick it in the mailbox. Your actions will brighten more lives than you could imagine. One man kept such a letter in his Bible for ten years!

Recently an Air Force captain wrote a simple letter to the head of the housekeeping department, expressing his gratefulness for their good work. One of the workers stopped him on the street and asked if he was the man who wrote that letter. She excitedly told him how the only letters they get are complaints! Thankfulness bubbled out of her, because someone noticed that she was trying to do the best she could.

George Washington set aside time each day to write letters. Almost all the founding fathers of our country regularly corresponded with people around the world. They communicated their ideas skillfully, with the desire to advance sound reasoning and truth.

You could follow in their footsteps. You could be a man who writes truth to people everywhere. But before you begin to write discourses on history, botany, or medical practices like Thomas Jefferson wrote, try learning to write a simple letter of encouragement. Once you try it you will be hooked for life! When you see the excitement and joy that a few words can bring, you will never underestimate the value of a letter.

One trick to writing letters is to get all your supplies ready before you need them. Find a drawer or a box and put some paper, envelopes, a pen, and a few stamps there. It's discouraging to try to write a letter and spend an hour looking for your tools. By then you are out of time and sometimes out of inspiration. At the local post office you can find some masculine stamps. It will cost a little to get set up, but everything worthwhile has a price.

I've given you a picture of what a letter can do. You've received a few practical tips. You've been given the example of the founding fathers. All that is left is for you to write a simple letter of encouragement. You'll be amazed at the results.

Happy writing!

> ***And I beseech you, bretheren, suffer the word of exhortation: for I have written a letter unto you in a few words*** (Hebrews 13:22).

Questions

- What tools do you need to write and send a letter?

- What are the elements of a simple letter of encouragement?

- Do you know any letters that the apostle Paul wrote? Luke? John?

- Do you like to get letters?

- Can you think of someone that you could write to today?

In order to secure a right home atmosphere for their children, parents themselves must be right.

—H. Clay Trumbull

Preparing for Your Children

On January 11, 1978, God gave us our first child. That evening my wife went to bed early. Our daughter Molly lay beside me on the couch. I watched her like any new dad would, thoroughly amazed that she belonged to me. I knew that I was responsible for her life. She was under my care, to protect, to provide for, and to train. Never having children before, I felt somewhat overwhelmed. "What will become of her life?" I wondered. I purposed at that moment to plan her education.

I picked up my Bible. Beginning in Proverbs, I read, looking for things to teach her. After an hour I was getting nowhere. I couldn't put my random thoughts into any sort of plan. "God," I asked, "what do I teach my daughter?"

He gently answered in my heart, "Be what you want her to be." I didn't expect that answer. I was thinking about molding her; God was thinking about molding me. "She will be what you are, not what you try to teach her."

How does this apply to you? It may be many years before you have children. Why should you consider your future children when there is baseball to play and trees to climb? If you wait until you have children before you consider training them, you will be years behind and may never catch up.

How old are you? When your children are your age, how will you want them to act? Your children will tend to act just the way you act. Are you honest? Are you a good worker? Do you complain? They will follow your example. There are exceptions and God is merciful. He doesn't always give us everything that we deserve. Not all of your poor traits will be passed on to your children; still, your children will tend to be what you are.

It is like God's law for trees. This law is just as sure as the law of gravity. The law of the trees states that an apple tree produces apples and peach trees produce peaches. It is a simple law. That law carries over into the lives of people. The children you produce will be like you. When your son is twelve years old, he will tend to act the same way you acted at twelve. If you are a grateful boy, you will tend to produce grateful children. If you are lazy, you will tend to produce lazy children. If you are respectful toward your parents, you will tend to produce respectful children. It is one of God's laws of life.

To some degree you chart the courses for your children and your grandchildren by every choice you make. Here is an exaggerated example. Suppose that your ball rolls out into the road. In the excitement of your game, you run out to get it without looking for cars. A large truck gets to the ball at the same time you do. An action like that today could prevent you from having children tomorrow.

Choices and actions that seem less significant will still affect the personalities of your children. If you diligently learn to play an instrument, your children will tend to play an instrument. A daddy who knows how to play the piano will tend to give his son or daughter a bent in that direction. Any subject that you master and make a part of your life, your children will pick up just by being with you. They will feel your excitement for it. Your example will display its daily usefulness.

The attitudes and habits that you are developing today will have an effect upon the man you become. The man you become will affect the future of your children.

It is easy to think that the things we do today don't have much bearing on the future. "I'm just a boy," you might say. "I will deal with that when I grow up." But a strange thing happens in life. You grow up before you realize it, and you are still doing the things that you did when you were young. If you don't change today, you have less chance of ever changing tomorrow.

I am trying to give you a vision—the vision of thinking like a man while you are still in the body of a boy. This vision will give you wisdom and understanding. It will add years to your life. It will help you to avoid many sorrows, promote healthy relationships, and gain true riches. The vision is this: What you do today will affect your world tomorrow. Every day that goes by, your character is hardened like a concrete slab. Your good character is solidified and your faults are made firm. Allowing poor habits and thoughts to run your life will burden the next generation. Developing good habits and thoughts is like putting blessings into a bank account for your children.

Understanding this lesson while you are young will give you a great jump on life and avoid many pitfalls. Boys can change easier than old men. By earnestly taking responsibility for all of your actions, you can break away from poor habits and concentrate on good ones. Take an honest look at your life. Ask your parents or your friends to point out your faults and strengths. Call out to God to make you into the man you know you should be. Begin changing today. Never let up on becoming that man until the day you die.

If you set out to live a cheerful, productive boyhood, you can be confident that your children will tend to do the same. They will tend to be cheerful sons and daughters that live and work just like Dad. You might ask, "How does that happen when they are not here now to see me?" All I can say is that it is just a part of God's laws for living. Good trees produce good fruit. Life is not just some chance happening.

God reserves the right to do anything He wants. Sometimes we cannot understand why things happen. However, most of life is very predictable. Good trees produce good fruit. A boy that lives according to God's judgments and statutes today will harvest a crop of good children in the future.

Therefore, when you are tempted to do something foolish, when you feel like breaking the rules, consider that your actions will be repeated in a generation to come. Instead, purpose to live today like a man who is laying a foundation for future generations. Not only will this perspective tend to give you a life without regrets, it will be a safeguard to your children and grandchildren, should God ever give you that great blessing.

The Lord is longsuffering, and of great mercy, forgiving iniquity and transgression, and by no means clearing the guilty, visiting the iniquity of the fathers upon the children unto the third and fourth generation

(Numbers 14:18).

Questions

- Why should a young boy think about having children?

- What can you do to prepare for training your children?

- Why do you want to work on having good habits when you are young?

- What is the law of trees? How does that law relate to people?

- Do you have a poor habit that you need to change today?

Resources

Johannes Kepler, by John Hudson Tiner, Mott Media

Self Help, by Samuel Smiles, Bernard Palissy's life story

7 minutes with God, NavPress

How to Spend a Day in Prayer, NavPress

Made in the USA
Middletown, DE
06 September 2024

60486090R00126